LEADER'S GUIDE

Leader's Guide to Small Groups Using the *Proven Women Workbook Study*.

by Joel Hesch, Founder of Proven Men Ministries, Ltd. and
Emily Woody, Co-author of *Proven Women*.

This is your step-by-step Leader's Guide for equipping you to form and conduct a small group using the companion *Proven Women Workbook Study*. Each woman separately works through the *Study* during the week and the group gathers weekly to discuss what they have learned, receive additional training, and openly share struggles and victories. Small groups are encouraged because a *PROVEN*™ life requires open and vulnerable relationships with others, and this guide helps you equip others with the necessary tools to stand firm and join the sisterhood of *PROVEN Women*.

The battle for sexual integrity is fierce. Each woman must be constantly on guard. This *Leader's Guide* provides you with the tools necessary to teach others to be victorious.

The name Proven was derived from our acrostic PROVEN WOMEN™ and stands for women who are stamped "Proven" by the Lord because they are striving to be:

Passionate for God,
Repentant in spirit,
Open and honest,
Victorious in living,
Eternal in perspective, and
Networking with other *PROVEN Women.*™

Thank you for accepting the invitation to become connected with us and join our team in helping develop other Proven Women.

Copyright © 2021 by Joel Hesch

All rights reserved. No part of this book may be reproduced in any form or electronic or mechanical means without permission in writing from the author, except by a reviewer, who may quote brief passages in a review. Contact information: info@ProvenMen.org.

Published and printed in the U.S.A. by Proven Men Ministries, Ltd., Lynchburg, Virginia

First Edition

ISBN: 978-1-940011-22-6

Proven Women, Proven Woman, Proven Men, Proven Man, Proven Path, Proven Life, and the PROVEN term and acronym are protected trademarks and service marks of Joel Hesch.

Scripture taken from the HOLY BIBLE, NEW INTERNATIONAL VERSION. NIV. Copyright © 1973, 1978, 1984 by International Bible Society.

Used by permission of Zondervan Publishing House. All rights reserved.

Details in stories or anecdotes have been changed to protect the identities of the persons involved. Interior Design:

Cover Design: 1106 Design

Hesch, Joel

Leader's Guide to Small Groups Using the Proven Women Workbook Study.

1. Sex—Religious aspects—Christianity. 2. Temptation. 3. Christian women—Religious life. 4. Sexual Health Recovery.

TABLE OF CONTENTS

Preface: The PROVEN Model for Small Groups v

I. Introduction 1

II. Who Should Lead a Proven Group? 3

III. Beginning the Process of Forming a Proven Group 5
    Prayer 5
    Husbands 6
    Selecting a Co-leader 7
    Obtaining Church Leadership Support 7
    Knowing the Materials 8

IV. Scheduling a Group 9
    Day, Time and Place for Meetings 9
    Determining the Size of the Group 11
    Making the Announcement 11

V. Selecting Members 13
    Don't "Convince" Anyone to Join 14
    Repeat Attenders 15
    Bondage to Other Sins 15

VI. Structure of Small Group Meetings 17
    The Role of Leaders During Meetings 19
    Confidentiality and Other Ground Rules 21
    Dealing with Difficulties in Meetings 23
        Time Hogs 24
        Biblically Incorrect Statements and Irrelevant Discussions 24
        Silent Participants 25

VII. The Meetings 29

VIII. Helping Non-group Members 33

IX. Life After Group 35

X. Training Future Group Leaders 37

XI. Using These Materials for Regular Women's Groups 39

XII. Conclusion 41
Appendix A: Sample Ground Rules 43
Appendix B: Detailed Leader's Guides for All Group Meetings 45
    Week 1 47
    Week 2 61
    Week 3 71
    Week 4 81
    Week 5 89
    Week 6 97
    Week 7 105
    Week 8 113
    Week 9 121
    Week 10 129
    Week 11 137
    Week 12 145
    Week 13 151

Preface
The PROVEN™ Model for Small Groups

You can lead others into breaking free from the grip of sexual sins and to experiencing lasting freedom in Christ. This *Leader's Guide* shows you how to position others to receive God's healing and be changed from the inside out. Proven groups begin by embracing and applying the following six essential components of a Proven life:

P – Passionate for God. As you take your attention off yourself and your rights and circumstances and focus on the Lord, you will discover the perfection and goodness of God, who deserves to be praised. Your newfound passion for the Lord will replace your lust for selfish desires and practices. During times of intimate worship, you will receive God's very nature and experience His healing in all areas of your life.

R – Repentant in Spirit. Until you see that your conduct is evil because it separates you from closeness to God, you won't truly want to change. Repentance is not self-manufactured, and it means more than merely having feelings of guilt or shame. Rather, it is a gift from God, granted to those who humbly seek Him with all their hearts. As you confess each of your sins and submit to the Lord, you will be restored and renewed.

O – Open and Honest. One of the main reasons people turn to false forms of intimacy, such as pornography, masturbation, or fantasy, is to keep from being vulnerable. If you have been hurt in relationships, you will probably try to hide from open, vulnerable relationships. However, your heart and soul inwardly long for true intimacy. Fortunately, God will enable you to trust again. He will guide you to be open, permit feelings to return, and engage in fulfilling and genuine relationships.

V – Victorious in Living. You cannot overcome temptation and sin in your own strength. You must join God's winning team, and when you remain in His camp, you'll lead a victorious life. Each moment you yield to the Lord and rely upon His power, your actions will become pure and holy, as He is pure and holy.

E – Eternal in Perspective. When dwelling on the temporary (your present circumstances), you act according to immediate thoughts and desires. Taking on an eternal perspective, on the other hand, brings hope and perseverance during temptations and trials. By looking to God's promises and allowing the Holy Spirit to be your guide, you will live out peace and joy in all circumstances. You will no longer be worn out from chasing after temporary pleasures or defeated from the constant battle of trying to control life.

N – Networking with Other *PROVEN* Women. You were created for relationships, first with God and next with others. True networking, seeking out and engaging with others on a vulnerable level, provides a way of living out your real purposes. Other *Proven Women* are also a great source of encouragement. Two *Proven Women* are as iron sharpening iron.

# Introduction

You are to be commended for desiring to lead a small group and point others in the direction of freedom from bondage to sexual sins. There are plenty of women who need to link together with someone who has an encouraging and non-judgmental heart. This gives you an incredible opportunity to minister to the women in your group.

There are a couple of things that you must accept before leading a small group. First, you cannot rescue your fallen sister; and second, you cannot make anyone live out purity and righteousness. No matter how enthusiastic you are, and regardless of what truth you possess, you won't convince others to hate sexual sins or to love the Lord with all their hearts. Just as salvation does not result from fine-sounding arguments (1 Corinthians 1:17), deliverance from bondage to sexual sins (and moving toward sexual integrity) is not gained by following the latest program (Colossians 2:20–23). Spiritual battles can only be won through prayer, by relying upon the Lord, and in using the weapons God provides (Ephesians Chapter 6). As a fellow soldier, though, you can remind others of the Lord's battle plan and encourage them through your example as you obey God's commands. Your sacred duty will be to pray for the women in your group. You will also be asked to show the love of Christ to them.

In short, the goal of a *Proven Women Study* small group is to position each woman to be healed by God through a deepening intimate love relationship with the Lord so that they experience the joy of walking victoriously in God's power and in unity with Him. As a facilitator, you will inspire group members primarily by living out holiness and being devoted to them. When you model a Proven life (Passion, Repentance, Openness, Victorious living, Eternal perspective, and Networking) you can anticipate seeing them become Proven Women.

The companion *Proven Women Study* is also well suited for women who don't greatly struggle with sexual purity but desire to grow deeper with the Lord and live out a Proven life. As explained in Chapter XI, successful women's groups have used these materials as Bible studies. Although this guide utilizes a small recovery framework for most of the discussion, the same principles apply to general women's studies and groups.

 # Who Should Lead a Proven Group?

You don't need to be a trained minister to lead a Proven Women group. Many of the best group leaders are ordinary Christian women who have faced difficult struggles and are now living a victorious life (2 Corinthians 1:3–5). In fact, women who continually struggle with sexual sins really want to know that the group leader can identify with their struggles. You should expect that some women will think that God's grace is reserved for others and that they are left alone to struggle throughout life. Your *humble* example will help open their eyes to the same hope and victory offered to all women who turn to the Lord. Although speaking from experience can be very helpful, that doesn't mean you need to have been a sexual sinner to lead this type of group. If you have a heart panting after God and compassion for women struggling with sexual sins, then you more than qualify—even if it has been a dozen years since you last looked at pornography or masturbated.

> Women who continually struggle with sexual sins want to know that the group leader can really identify with their struggles.

To lead a group, you must sincerely relate to their struggles and be walking a victorious life. Although there are no hard or fast rules, generally a leader should be free from sexual bondage for about one year and should be well equipped and accustomed to wearing God's armor. This is because there will be increased temptations in your life once you become a leader of this type of a group. Satan knows that if he can get you, the group will be weakened. You must be prepared to meet these battles in the power of the Lord.

To be an effective leader, you must be able to accept constructive criticism and recognize your own limitations. God works mightily in a humble heart. He will constantly reveal more truth to you and impart wisdom if your heart remains soft and your eyes are fixed upon Him.

As you keep putting into practice each of the elements of the *PROVEN* acronym, you will grow as a godly leader and see the Lord working in your life and the lives of those in your group.

When you give up your selfish ambitions and totally yield to Christ out of sincere love and thanksgiving, you'll be able to properly do His work. It is then that Galatians 2:20 becomes real in your life. It is then that you learn to know and do His will. It is then that you are able to be God's hands and touch others. Even after you become a group leader, keep asking the Lord to humble and guide you. Keep looking to Him for healing in your life, and keep petitioning the Lord to give mercy and grace to the women you lead.

Rest assured, when the Lord calls you to lead a group, He will light the way. With His strength and wisdom, you can effectively minister to others. This *Leader's Guide* is designed to be a resource to help you form and run a small support group. Of course, the Holy Spirit should be your main teacher and guide. Lean not on your own understanding or strength, but remain a needy, dependent servant of the Lord, and He will guide you and work in the lives of the women you seek to serve (Proverbs 3:5–6).

III Beginning the Process of Forming a Proven Group

There are many things that need to occur before you publicly announce the formation of a small group. Your attention to the following five preliminary items will make a big difference as to whether the group is successful. Don't take shortcuts.

PRAYER

Prayer is the most important aspect of any ministry, especially with respect to the spiritual battles involved in sexual sin. You will need to be in daily prayer before and while leading a small group. In fact, prayer is our way of relating to God. The only way that you will know and carry out God's will is by first knowing Him. And the only way you will remain walking in victory is to remain dependent upon the Lord. Similarly, the women you seek to guide won't be healed because they attend a group. The spiritual battles they face will only be won through humbly moving God into action through prayer and obedience. Therefore, prayer must be the top priority in your life, and you must set an example for others to follow. Consider reading a book on prayer, such as *The Circle Maker: Praying Circles Around Your Biggest Dreams and Greatest Fears,* by Mark Batterson. Ask your pastor for other suggestions.

> Prayer must be the top priority in your life, and you must set an example for others to follow.

HUSBANDS

Married women, is your husband on board? Is he fully supportive? Be sure to have plenty of heart-to-heart talks with him. He will be affected. For instance, he may be reluctant for you to take a visible role because some people will likely judge you, his wife. He is rightfully aware that some will be thinking you give in to pornography based solely upon your connection to a purity group. His concerns are valid. Not everyone in church will think or act in a godly manner. However, by God's strength, you both will stand up under trials.

If your husband is not in full support, then stay in prayer asking the Lord to reveal to you whether there is anything in your life that is a hindrance to his support. Be sure to search whether you are motivated by pride in leading other women. In addition, openly and honestly evaluate if you have truly demonstrated brokenness over your sexual and other relational sins and have sought full restoration in your relationship with your spouse. Listen to your husband and find out why he is reluctant. He will have meaningful insights. Ask him if he senses that you still have a problem with pride or whether he fears that you will stumble once you establish yourself as a target for Satan by standing as an example of a woman walking in purity. Again, if you are walking in your own strength, you will fall.

After asking God to search your heart and acting upon what He shows you, if your spouse is still reluctant, begin asking the Lord to change his heart. Be patient and wait upon the Lord. When God calls, you will be able to follow. He won't call you without also leading your spouse to support you.

Your husband's role in the overall process is important for other reasons. In fact, an intimate relationship with him will be a model for others. Keep monitoring whether you are paying attention to his needs, maintaining open and honest communications, and being gentle and sensitive. Do these things not because others are watching, but out of genuine love for the Lord and for your spouse. By continuing to live by the Holy Spirit, you will remain a woman worth following—both for your friends and for the women you want to lead.

SELECTING A CO-LEADER

If this is your first group, consider asking a spiritually sound woman with a soft heart and a passion for the Lord to co-lead with you. You will enjoy the support. Lay ministry is not easy, and there will be many bumps in the road. Don't forget, the Lord sent out the disciples two by two (Mark 6:7). Sharing the responsibility of leading the group and contributing to their spiritual growth may develop a close friendship with your co-leader. At the very least, you must have an accountability partner with whom you can openly discuss your walk with the Lord, including any temptations or struggles you face. In fact, the lack of accountability is a major factor in church leaders falling.

OBTAINING CHURCH LEADERSHIP SUPPORT

The greatest fear some women have is that others, and especially the church, will judge them. This is a huge obstacle in women being willing to contact you about sexual integrity or joining a group. Some women may have believed that all of their sexual temptations and struggles would immediately disappear when they accepted Christ as their Savior or when they got married. Because they continue to commit sexual sins, they may think that they are defective or wonder if they are the only Christian with this struggle. For these women, the intense shame often leads to even heavier reliance upon coping mechanisms such as fantasy, pornography or masturbation, which, ironically, are the very things of which they are ashamed. This downward cycle of despair is not easily broken. Therefore, never lose sight of the fact that there is so much guilt wrapped up in sexual sin, especially for a Christian, that it can be extremely difficult for women who are caught in these struggles to think that the church will not judge them. For many, it seems safer to just keep the sin hidden than to risk judgment. When they see others, such as yourself, admit sexual struggles and they trust that the church leadership is committed to providing a safe source of healing, the walls begin to crumble, and healing begins in their hearts and lives.

> Plan how to seek and obtain support from church leadership, including the pastors and leaders of the women's ministry.

Don't just expect that your pastor has experience in effectively addressing sexual sins. He may not know the long road that is often required for lasting freedom. Plan how to seek and obtain support from church leadership, including the pastors and leaders of the women's ministry. Before beginning a group at your church, you must meet with certain key leaders. You should ensure that they support your vision and approach. They must also be gently convinced of issues involved in the healing process. Approach the head pastor initially and let him know you want to form a small group modeled after the Proven materials. Share with him your heart and your desire to live out a Proven life and to lead others toward sexual integrity. Listen to his views regarding the healing path for those who struggle with pornography, fantasy, or masturbation. Ask him to read this *Leader's Guide* and to visit the website of ProvenWomen.org. Plan on having more than one conversation with him. Give him time to realize the great need for this ministry and to see that you are ready to lead the way. It can be hard for a pastor to swallow, but most churchgoers struggle with some form of lust, such as pornography, masturbation or fantasy. In some churches, it is believed to be nearly three-fourths of the congregation. The problem is real, and it needs a real solution. We cannot make it go away by trying harder to keep sexual sins a secret. In fact, keeping the topic taboo only reinforces the guilt and shame that leads many to try escaping into still more fantasy and into a further flight from true intimacy. Open and honest communication regarding sexual sin is sorely needed in the church. Without it, healing will not result. The question is, will your church be known as a place where sexual sinners are neither ignored nor told to simply pray about it, and will it become a leader in providing a safe place of openness and healing?

Once your head pastor understands that you are asking to be part of the solution to a very real problem in his church and that you are volunteering for front-line duty, he will most likely embrace your ministry and support your efforts to hold small groups. After the head pastor is on board, ask him for help informing other appropriate leaders and obtaining their support. Be willing to include other women in the process. You'll be blessed to have others share the load. Besides, it's not about you leading so much as it is about the Lord being glorified by the living sacrifices of women living out holy and faithful lives (Romans 12:1–2).

At some point, you will want the head pastor to make some form of an endorsement of the group from the pulpit. The church must be seen as a place of healing and recovery from sexual sins. The open support of the pastor is very important. It need not be anything more than you making an announcement one Sunday morning during church service and the pastor stating something to the effect that he has reviewed the materials and hopes every woman, including church leaders, would join the group. It could also be a form of endorsement in the bulletin or church website.

KNOWING THE MATERIALS

It's important that you know the materials you will be using in your group. For instance, you should have spent twelve weeks in the *Proven Women Study* at least once, if not more. You should also read any other suggested Proven books. Your knowledge of these materials will help sharpen your eternal perspective and demonstrate your capability and commitment to lead.

Scheduling a Group

After receiving support and approval from church leaders, there are a few logistical matters to attend to before actually starting a group. First, have plenty of copies of the *Proven Study* on hand or instruct the women to order them. Next, give careful thought to the location, time, and size of the small group meetings. Each of these things makes a difference. Even the timing and the manner in which you announce the group can influence a positive or negative response. The logistics are very important and must be well planned out.

DAY, TIME AND PLACE FOR MEETINGS

The start date and day of the week must be carefully selected. There are two times of the year that are particularly good points to begin: (1) in mid-September, beginning after school starts and ending before Christmas; and (2) mid-January, after the holidays are over. Summer can be too hectic to try to find twelve weeks free from vacations or nights filled with family activities. Regardless of when you run the first group meeting, plan ahead for the next one for those who tell you that they cannot make it now but want to know if and when it will be offered again. Expect that groups, especially the first one, will be small. Don't be discouraged. Even if you are used by God to change just one life, it's worth it. Besides, just like teaching any Bible study, leading a small Proven group will bless you as much as it blesses others. Moreover, as stated below, a smaller group is usually more effective.

The day of the week on which meetings are held is an important consideration. While the wishes of potential members are important, you must ultimately decide the day. Begin by evaluating whether you have just one day of the week that you can protect or if you can be flexible, depending on the needs of those signing up. It must be a day that you and your co-leader will be able to keep every week. For instance, if you travel for work but can almost always be at home on Monday nights, then pre-select Mondays. Those who cannot attend on Mondays because they have a college class or other events will need to rearrange their schedules or wait until the next group.

Even if your day of the week is flexible, you may find that each woman has a preference vastly different from the others. Some women are reluctant to give up Saturday mornings because that day is spent on children's activities. Others might have classes or exercise routines three nights a week. You cannot cater to each woman's schedule, and ultimately, you will have to select a day knowing that it will preclude some from attending. That's okay. Let them know that you will be holding the same study again in the future and that there will be plenty of time to arrange their schedules.

You should hold twelve to fourteen weekly meetings. Between meetings, it is strongly suggested to have some form of contact with each woman, whether by email or telephone. It doesn't need to be a long conversation, but it should be personal. Tell them you are praying for them and ask if they have specific requests or anything to share, whether struggles or victories.

The time of the meetings is also a factor. Meetings should last two hours. You can be somewhat flexible on the time of the meetings, and even alter it slightly, once the group is formed. Just make sure that a specific time becomes fixed and that each person commits to making it a top priority to arrive on time.

Once you decide upon a day and time, it's important that you develop a schedule and make it clearly known to those desiring to attend the group. You will be asking them to commit to making these dates a top priority. By actually recording the exact dates for the twelve weeks, you underscore their importance, and you will also be able to foresee any problem dates, such as a holiday or a conflicting church function. If one of the dates falls on a holiday or there is another reason that a meeting cannot be held, schedule it ahead of time as a night off. As that date approaches, remind the women in the group of the off night, but stress that it does not reduce the importance of the daily *Heartwork* during that time. You may also want to increase your outside contact with them because two weeks is a long time away from face-to-face accountability and support.

> When selecting a location, be sensitive and maintain confidentiality.

The location needs to be a place where you can control the privacy of the meetings. You may meet in your home if you have a private area. You can also meet at a room owned by the church, provided you can ensure privacy. When selecting a location, be sensitive and maintain confidentiality. Guard against parading women through places they will be forced to encounter others from church. Over time, however, many women will drop their guard and even tell others that they are in the group. Regardless, be a protector of their confidences, even in selecting a particular room or location.

DETERMINING THE SIZE OF THE GROUP

Smaller groups are better than larger groups. You want women to feel connected, have enough time to share inner feelings, and practice open communication regarding difficult topics. The group should be small enough that each woman can pour out her heart to the Lord and engage in personal discussions. Often, the best size is between two and six, not including the leaders, although it is possible to hold larger groups. If you have more than eight or ten women desiring to join a small group, consider holding two groups or ask some to wait until the next session.

MAKING THE ANNOUNCEMENT

After completing all of the above pre-flight work, you are ready to announce the formation of a small group.

Regardless of your excitement or your willingness to openly share your testimony or the nature of the group, you need to think about how your announcement will be perceived by two types of people: (1) those needing to be in the group; and (2) others, including their friends and spouses. A common mistake in first starting a small group is to make it sound like a meeting for recovering sex addicts. This scares off many who would otherwise want to be in the group. It also sets the wrong tone for the focus of the group. In addition, a spouse might tell his wife that he does not want her being associated with a "sex addict" group and discourage her from joining. You can have the right intention but fail to be sensitive to the needs and feelings of both groups. In your announcements, focus upon the aspects of sexual integrity, desiring purity and walking in holiness.

Also, emphasize the notion that this group is open to those who want to mentor others in the area of holiness and purity. Thus, people who may be prone to judge won't know if those in your group are ministering or being ministered to.

There are many ways to get the word out, including announcements in the church bulletin, discussions at existing women's groups, or using email. Be sure to clear any announcement with the church leadership before making it. Again, it's very important to gain the full support of the head pastor or even a public endorsement from him or references to the group from the pulpit. For many, if they do not hear the pastor suggest something, they are afraid to get involved. He has an influence in their lives that you do not.

Once you succeed in getting your pastor's full support and understanding of the importance of the group, you may find that he even mentions some aspect of the group in sermons when talking about brokenness, holiness, or the healing power of God.

> Women need time to really think about whether the benefits outweigh the risks. It may take several times hearing of your group before they respond.

Plan to begin making announcements at least four to five weeks before the start date of your group. Some women will be on vacation or away from church the day you begin your announcement. In addition, it often takes three times hearing an announcement for someone to act upon it, so make three or four announcements. If your church doesn't permit announcements, use bulletin inserts, website notices, or social media posts if they do allow any of these. (Again, get prior approval from the head pastor before making any announcement.)

Be sure to start planning early. Women need time to really think about whether the benefits outweigh the risks. It may take several times hearing of your group before they respond.

# Selecting Members

Selecting members is important. Not everyone who expresses an interest is ready to commit to this type of a group, and not everyone should be in your group.

After making announcements, you will likely have women mention something to you on Sunday morning as you gather for church. There are many reasons why women speak to you at this time. Seeing you may remind them of the need to talk to you, or they may not have wanted to call you during the week for fear that their husbands might overhear them. Normally, this is not the best time to talk in detail about the group. First, you want to be preparing your heart for worship. Second, you want to be available to meet and greet others who may want to know more about the group. Finally, you may not have the time or ability to concentrate on them. Therefore, you need to get their telephone number or email address.

Whenever you have an initial discussion, let them know that the group is for those who desire sexual integrity, purity and holiness. You may also want to suggest that they read the www.ProvenWomen.org website. You have freedom to share more information as time and setting permit, such as the primary focus of the group being upon purity and sexual integrity, and generally talking about the type of group that will be held. Be sure to put them at ease, and avoid sounding like you are beyond temptation or are the expert on the topic. Let them know it is a safe place to share and grow in dealing with a subject that many women battle.

Be mindful that it is very difficult for some women to approach you or admit problems. Some women think that they are the only ones who masturbate, and others may have vowed never to confide in anyone. Your reaction and warm invitation can help untie the knot that holds them in secrecy. Thus, if possible, weave into your discussion that you are so broken over your own sins that you won't judge them, no matter what specific sins they have committed.

When the ministry was first formed, leaders would meet for over an hour with each woman, essentially going over what is now the content of the first meeting. It was a screening process, as well as an attempt to connect with each woman. However, the modern trend is to have a short, encouraging discussion with those expressing an interest in the group. Almost every woman who asks to join is invited to attend the first meeting where they get their first taste of being open with other women. We have discovered that asking the women to openly share in a safe group environment is a terrific first step for breaking down some of the walls that keep them in bondage. They are encouraged to see other women in similar positions. They also become connected to others in the group by this process. Be sure, however, to inform each woman that she will be asked to be open and share her story so she won't be totally caught off guard.

Plan to review the detailed meeting guide in Appendix B in order to get an appreciation for how the first meeting is conducted. For instance, you will note that the leader shares her story and then invites each woman to do the same. It also suggests a particular method of explaining the cause and cure for addiction and for encouraging women to make commitments. Plan on using each word picture and analogy in your first group meeting, because they help set the stage for understanding the cause and cure for sexual struggles. In addition, you will be able to refer to these word pictures in future group meetings.

DON'T "CONVINCE" ANYONE TO JOIN

Never press a woman to join a group. In fact, don't try to convince anyone to join. It needs to be the right timing for each woman, and each woman must be willing to do whatever it takes for healing to occur. You will regret "convincing" someone to attend, because she will not be ready to be healed and will likely disrupt the rest of the group.

> You will regret "convincing" someone to attend, because she will not be ready to be healed and will likely disrupt the rest of the group.

In fact, it's unfair to the others for you to allow someone into your group who needs to be constantly convinced of her sin, openly shifts blame, or argues each point you try to teach. The group will digress into a debate instead of a place to meet with and be healed by God. Always remember that your role is to be available to minister to those ready to receive God's healing and to provide a safe atmosphere where that can be accomplished. It's not your job to plead with anyone to join the group or to convince them to give up their sins. If they are not ready, they should not be in the group. Those who are not ready now can always join a later group. Of course, this does not mean that you can never initiate a conversation about the group or ask women to consider it. Certainly, you should make announcements at women's meetings and other forums. Also, if you have an established relationship with a woman or if anyone has expressed an interest in the group before, then you can gently inquire as to whether they might be interested.

REPEAT ATTENDERS

Twelve weeks may be enough for some women to be set on a path toward walking in victory. For others, however, it's too short a time period. Therefore, it's a good idea to consider permitting some women to repeat the group as space permits, provided that they are committed. There is so much packed in the twelve weeks that it will still be fresh and exciting the second (or third or fourth) time through. In fact, as discussed below, you should encourage all of the women to redo the *Study* with another woman.

BONDAGE TO OTHER SINS

On occasion, women who are in bondage to other sins will ask to join the group because they want to live a Proven life. Although other women in the group may initially feel uncomfortable sharing sexual sins while another woman confesses another sin, if the person is really ready to do business with God and devote herself to healing, it could be a good idea to allow her to participate. However, you must meet with that woman and carefully evaluate whether she is humble and teachable. You will need to be sensitive at each meeting and regularly remind the woman addressing the non-sexual sins the necessity for sensitivity, vulnerability, and loyalty to the group. Remind her that others could feel uncomfortable, especially if she never shares difficult struggles or if she is not vulnerable with her own weaknesses and sins. In short, there can be a place for women who want purity and holiness in all areas of their lives, because all forms of sin stem in some way from a common root issue of pride and selfishness. Each woman has much in common with others, and the healing path is the same for anyone desiring to be pure and stamped Proven by God.

Passionate for God,
Repentant in spirit,
Open and honest,
Victorious in living,
Eternal in perspective, and
Networking with other *Proven Women.*

Structure of Small Group Meetings

You will find a detailed guide to each weekly meeting in Appendix B. This is designed to help you structure your group, and make you feel comfortable leading even if you've never led a meeting before. Plan to review Appendix B to get a feel for the structure of the group. Below is some additional guidance on leading group meetings. As an initial matter, you need to encourage the women to attend every meeting and to be on time. It's your responsibility, however, to end on time. Show discipline and respect by never running late. Delete some discussion if you have to, but end on time. If they choose to stick around and visit in the parking lot, that's fine, but the meetings themselves should have set beginning and ending times. Be sure that each meeting contains all of the elements of the *PROVEN* acronym, listed below:

P – Passionate for God. Meetings should always begin and end in prayer. They should also have other elements of praise and passionate worship, such as singing a song and thanking the Lord for His mercy. Each week, pick a song for the group to listen to together. This can be played through your phone or speaker. If you want, you can bring a copy of the lyrics for the ladies or ask them to look up the lyrics on their phones. If you play the song loud enough and have the words to follow along, all of the women will join in and sing. This is a wonderful way of bonding with each other, being open, and worshiping the Lord together.

R – Repentant in Spirit. Make it clear that the women are encouraged to confess sin and seek repentance during each meeting. Tell the women that they should let you know anytime they want to confess sin and ask for forgiveness, and let them know that it is even okay to raise their hands and ask. Never seek to fabricate repentance, but provide opportunities for it. In addition, set an example by making confessions. The women in your group will only be as open as you are! During most meetings, gently ask if anyone has recently stumbled. Finally, during closing prayers, each woman should be allotted time to pray. By following your example, they will often confess sin and pour out their hearts to the Lord in prayer. Therefore, guard the prayer time each week.

O – Open and Honest. Openness is one key weapon against guilt, shame, and other relational blocking mechanisms that lead toward false intimacy. As a leader, you must model open, honest, and vulnerable communications. Discuss your failings. Also share your victories, because there needs to be an element of hope. The more open you are, the more open they will be. Similarly, if they sense that some topics are off-limits, they won't feel freedom in sharing certain things. Also, model openness in your relationship with your spouse and with others. Confess when you have given the silent treatment. Share how you have asked for forgiveness as well as how readily it was given. Some women need more training in areas such as fostering a healthy relationship with a spouse, developing good communication skills, and offering or receiving forgiveness. Therefore, be ready to give life examples, such as how to listen without trying to fix problems, openly communicate on sensitive topics, or stop a fight in progress.

V – Victorious in Living. Are you walking in victory? Do the women sense your excitement about the Lord? Do they want what you have? Tell the women that they are not recovering sex addicts but are, instead, children of God. We are to carry that name (His name) because of the righteousness of the Lord. The message is one of hope, not despair. God forgives us the moment we ask for forgiveness, not when we feel like we are worthy of it. We walk in victory each moment we are led by the Lord and cooperating with Him (Galatians 5:16). The key point is that victory comes by God's power, not our own (John 15:5).

E – Eternal in Perspective. By keeping an eternal perspective, each woman will experience and retain God's vision and hope for her life. In addition, an eternal focus will help give encouragement when setbacks happen. Remind the women not to throw in the towel but to take on the eternal perspective that the goal is to live intimately with God and to enjoy His righteousness. Setbacks can actually have the positive effect of motivating us to let go of self-effort and become even more repentant, needy, and dependent upon the Lord. Living out our purpose in life—to love God with all of our hearts and love our neighbor as ourselves—is what really matters and brings peace, joy, and meaning into our lives.

N – Networking with Other *PROVEN Women*. It is important that women bond and develop vulnerability and intimacy with each other. Again, we were created for relationships with God and with others. It is our hiding from genuine relationships that results in turning to false forms of intimacy, such as pornography, fantasies, and other sinful ways of avoiding transparency and authenticity in relationships. Therefore, it should be your goal to become true friends with others, without setting limitations or barriers. For instance, set a practice of hugging each woman at the start and conclusion of each meeting, and model this in outside relationships with other women as well. In addition, foster a team spirit. Consider using the word picture of a mountain-climbing team. Tell the women that we are all tied to the same rope and that if one falls, it affects the others. Convey that, at times, one woman in the group will be taking the lead in sharing exciting experiences with the Lord and at other times, the same person will be following the footsteps of another. Godly teamwork and camaraderie are true forms of networking. They will also help demonstrate why we should all make it a top priority to be at every meeting and to do the daily *Heartwork* assignments in the *Study*.

In addition to generally incorporating each Proven element, be prepared each week with the specific content of the meetings. There are definite goals to be accomplished in each meeting on the path to a new and Proven life. Stated another way, group meetings are far more than a place for women to meet to confess sins or offer kind words of encouragement. The *Proven Study* and weekly meetings are designed to position each woman to meet with and be changed by God. A detailed suggested outline for each week is included in Appendix B. You should feel free, though, to shape the weekly meetings around your specific group. In fact, you could spend half of the time during a particular meeting in confession, praise, and worship, including singing, praying, or taking turns reading from Psalms in the first person (i.e., listing the specific names of each woman in the group or the term "we" when the author speaks of himself or others). The meetings should not be you doing all of the speaking.

THE ROLE OF LEADERS DURING MEETINGS

One of your largest roles is to provide a place of safety and trust. You want to foster an atmosphere where the love of Christ is communicated and each member feels comfortable in sharing her pain and failings. It's not your responsibility, however, to bring healing to a woman or to break her denial. Avoid the temptation to convince or coerce a woman to change. Just as God doesn't move through shame or guilt to coerce others into accepting His free gift of eternal salvation, the Lord will not bless your shaming tactics even for the goal of urging another into living out a pure and holy life. Instead, God uses His unconditional love to draw women into intimate relationships with Him. It's through a growing relationship that He heals the deep scars in hearts and souls. Therefore, we must not shame our fellow servants to get them to step in line. For instance, avoid asking who did not do their weekly *Study*. As you go through the discussions, it will be obvious to you as a leader if anyone did not do her work; there is no need to single anyone out. Be an encourager by sharing how the Lord uses what you learn each week. Shame and guilt are some of the tools Satan uses as a means of tightening the grip of bondage. In contrast, show women how to receive God's love and respond to the Holy

> You want to foster an atmosphere where the love of Christ is communicated and each member feels comfortable in sharing her pain and failings.

Spirit—the keys to removing sin's noose. Pray for, love and encourage women, making them feel accepted and a part of the group.

Although you are responsible for keeping the right focus in your group, you should not hog all of the time in teaching. These are small groups, not lectures. Become a good listener and foster godly discussions. In doing so, you'll be sincere in caring for and training the women in your group. In addition, each woman will take ownership of a principle when she is led to realize it herself.

As the leader, you'll need to be prepared each week, having an objective in mind, but you'll also need to be flexible to the needs of each woman on any given week. You will hear the stories of each woman in your first meeting. Therefore, you can tailor your discussions. For instance, you may know if one woman has a great fear of abandonment or if another was abused as a child. However, you cannot allow the meetings to digress into chit-chat or become overly focused upon one person's particular circumstances. Be sure to incorporate the main points from each week into your meetings. Discussing portions of the weekly *Study* during the group meetings emphasizes the importance of each woman completing the daily *Heartwork*.

It's worth repeating that for the group to flourish, you must model vulnerability. Share details on how you deal with your spouse and others, including the good and the bad (e.g., times you encourage others spiritually and times you pick fights). Most women in your group will likely have a fear of true intimacy as well as a lack of skill in vulnerable, open communication. Your example will be helpful.

In addition, guard against comparing group members with each other or yourself. God's timing is perfect for each person. Let them know that there is no optimum time for healing and that it will look different for each person. Do, however, remind them that when you first began dealing with your own sin, it was a difficult and long battle. Tell them not to expect to be at the same spiritual level right now as someone who has been walking in God's healing for a long time. Continue to affirm and encourage each woman. Similarly, don't view yourself as an expert or someone who has arrived. If you merely tell others how to fix their own problems, you will thwart healing. In fact, a person must learn to see the problem and solution herself before she can grow. That's why it's often best to ask a good question rather than try to give a great answer to a problem. Although it takes time and patience for results to be seen, in the end, the women will be able to address the situations they encounter rather than becoming dependent upon you to tell them how to react when new problems surface.

Finally, be sure that you regularly pray for each person during the meetings. You'll be surprised how others will follow the way you pray. Some will begin praying specifically for the other women in the group. Pray from your heart, and don't be concerned about fancy words. Many women are afraid to pray in public because they don't think that they speak very well. If you find yourself praying to impress them, confess it as sin and ask for forgiveness. Paul told his spiritual children to model after him as he followed Christ (1 Corinthians 11:1). Being a leader is a big responsibility. In fact, whether you ask them to or not, your fellow group members will be following your example. Especially in your prayer life, strive for intimacy and desire to glorify God. Your prayers can and should be a conduit for the Lord's will to be accomplished. A solid prayer life will also equip you in training others to experience the same thing.

CONFIDENTIALITY AND OTHER GROUND RULES

It's important to provide group members with a few ground rules to follow, especially confidentiality, and guidelines regarding how to show respect and love during group meetings. These are important issues because each member must view the group setting as a safe place to share personal matters. Below are six recommended general ground rules.

(1) MAINTAINING STRICT CONFIDENTIALITY

Confidentiality is the most important ground rule. The women must agree that what is shared in the group stays in the group. Nothing will make a woman clam up more quickly than thinking her story will be made known to others. Make sure that the notion of confidentiality includes even the names of the group members. Tell each member that if they violate this confidence, they should humbly confess it and ask for forgiveness.

Expect that a church leader may ask you who is in the group. If you aren't prepared to give an answer, you might feel compelled to tell him. Therefore, plan ahead how you will respond. The best way to handle this situation is just to say that the group has agreed to protect the confidentiality of each member and that you must honor that promise. Chances are good that he will agree that he does not need to know. Also share how this might ruin the ability of you to lead a group or slow the healing of the women in the group. If he persists, you should tell him you need time to pray about it and seek wise counsel, such as from the head pastor or elders of your church, before sharing the names.

(2) TAKING RESPONSIBILITY FOR PERSONAL ACTIONS

Each person must realize that she alone is responsible for receiving healing from the Lord. You cannot do it for her. Similarly, they must understand that healing is a process with a purpose and that there are no shortcuts. Looking for a list of things to avoid or trusting a program to fix you will not produce lasting freedom (Colossians 2:20–23). Therefore, each woman must commit to making it a high priority to use the *Proven Study* each day to meet with the

Lord—who is the only one who can heal and change them. In doing so, however, she must humbly and willingly cooperate with God and rely upon His strength to overcome.

(3) ATTENDING GROUP

It's vital that each woman commits to attending each meeting. First, it's not fair to others if someone misses a meeting. Each woman in the group will have shared her deepest secrets and become vulnerable with the other women. A unique bond forms between the women, and when one woman is missing, the group dynamic is affected. Secondly, the woman who does not attend a particular meeting will miss out on valuable opportunities to practice being open, and she will miss out on learning important truths gained from group interaction and times of teaching.

Ask the women to make attending each and every meeting a high priority. They should commit to rearranging their schedules to avoid conflicts and to attend the meetings even when they are tired or do not feel like coming. If they simply cannot make a meeting, they should notify you in advance. In addition, each woman should commit to attending on time. If they must be late, tell them they should slip in quietly and not disrupt the meeting by announcing their presence and shaking hands. Be sure, however, to tell the women that it is better for them to arrive late, even if only for the last thirty minutes, than to miss group.

If a group member calls you to say she cannot be there, ask why. If she is tired or running late, encourage her to come anyway. Let her know that you are eager to see her and that the other women want her there too. Even if she can only attend the last fifteen minutes, it is worth it for her to come. We have had many women who told the leader they were too tired to come or that they would be very late if they did attend, and then end up telling the leaders they were so glad that they made the effort and arrived even for the prayer time at the end. In short, as a leader, you should lovingly encourage the women to attend.

(4) PARTICIPATING IN MEETINGS

If you are not diligent in running the meetings, some women will only share on a surface level or remain in a comfort zone they will not be willing to leave. Ask each woman to commit to working hard at recognizing and sharing feelings. To help them in this area, keep referring during meetings to the *Feelings Chart* in Appendix F of the companion *Proven Study*. Ask the women to commit to being open, real, and vulnerable while participating in discussions. Tell them that a common defense mechanism for avoiding intimacy is to bring up side issues, argue over disputable doctrines, or raise other matters, all of which take away from an atmosphere where everyone can share difficult personal issues and work toward a healing path. Ask them to commit to staying on topic and sharing from their hearts. For instance, tell the group in advance that if a discussion starts going down a rabbit trail, you will redirect the focus. Ask the women for their grace in allowing you to cut off distracting or unnecessary discussions.

(5) RESPECTING OTHERS

Remind the women that the group is just that: a group. It's important that it remains a place where all the women are able to grow and receive healing. It's also important that each woman show respect for the others, even those with difficult personalities. Ask each woman to agree to be mindful of any tendency she may have to dominate conversations or to monopolize discussions and sharing times. Those who are more vocal need to commit to limit their time so others have the same amount of time to share. In addition, each person must give undivided attention when another person is sharing. No one should interrupt, and similarly, no one should judge another group member.

(6) KEEPING EVIL OUT

As stated above, the group is to be a safe place. Therefore, no one should bring into the meetings things that may cause another to stumble. For instance, warn the women to avoid discussing unnecessary graphic details about sexual matters, which might be a trigger or a stumbling block for another woman. It's appropriate to confess that they viewed pornography, but it would not add anything to the discussion if they shared the particular details of the content to get the point across. It's important to maintain a balance in this regard.

Sample ground rules are attached as Appendix A. However, feel free to modify the ground rules to suit your particular group. It's not necessary for a person to sign an agreement.

DEALING WITH DIFFICULTIES IN MEETINGS

Dealing with difficult people will be one of your responsibilities. In gentle and loving ways, you can direct the group and even train others to respond maturely. It's possible to allow others to participate in the process of redirecting the group when distractions or disruptions occur. For instance, without shaming, you might ask others to comment on what a person in the group said. However, if you use this technique only when you want others to correct another, it will likely be misused. You must make sure that you don't teach others to use shaming techniques or permit women to attack each other. The group is to be a safe environment where openness is permitted and encouraged. However, it also provides a training ground for godly communication and intimacy, especially when teaching women how to improve communication. By viewing these difficulties as opportunities for growth, you'll keep from feeling defeated. Keep the proper perspective that the women need godly training and will only experience more and more of the nature of the Lord through trials and the refiner's fire. A few common types of situations that you must address are: (1) time hogs; (2) biblically incorrect statements and/or totally irrelevant discussions; and (3) silent participants.

TIME HOGS

Expect that at least one woman will want to do most of the talking or get the group to focus on her circumstances. After all, the same pride that ignited her flames of lust also fuels this self-centered behavior. Consider it a great opportunity to expose a woman's root issues to her and allow the woman to grow. One polite way of controlling an excessive talker is to periodically say things such as, "Let's hear from someone else," or "How about a view from someone who has not spoken?" At some point, you may need to talk to this person privately about the issue. If you properly set the stage by telling the group about the participation guidelines (see Appendix A), it will be easier to take charge in this situation. This is why you should establish ground rules at the first meeting. This allows you to remind a particular woman of the group's purpose and the ground rules in place. Privately ask her to be mindful of how much time she is using and the need for shy women to participate more. Tell her that some women won't talk until there is silence for a set amount of time, and ask her to give them room and time to participate. Remind her of the verse that says to be quick to listen and slow to speak (James 1:19). The key is to avoid a confrontational attitude and to reprove gently and with love. Always affirm while you give guidance or even a rebuke. Tell her of the positive changes that you are seeing in her life. If you do this lovingly and gently, you may win over a lifetime friend. However, if an excessive talker continues to disrupt the group after repeated cautions, you will have to set limits in greater ways. If it gets to the point that others no longer want to attend, you may even have to ask the woman to either remain silent during the meetings (except for the short time allotted for each woman during "check-in") or to stop attending.

BIBLICALLY INCORRECT STATEMENTS AND IRRELEVANT DISCUSSIONS

It is important that you develop a game plan for each meeting and guard against losing time and attention due to irrelevant topics. Time will always be a factor. A two-hour meeting will fly by quickly. In fact, it is doubtful that you can cover every one of the topics in the proposed schedules in Appendix B for weekly meetings. That's why you must prepare for and plan out your meetings in advance and be a good facilitator during group. Each meeting is designed to be a time of opening up to God and to His healing. It requires participation by each group member, and it's far more than a group of women meeting to talk about spiritual matters. The lessons are selected to foster growth in certain areas that are sorely lacking in most women who are running away from vulnerable intimacy.

Structure of Small Group Meetings

At times a person will say something that is simply incorrect, unscriptural, or irrelevant. For instance, a woman might suggest that it is okay to fantasize about sex for a few seconds without sinning because she is merely admiring God's creation. At other times, a person might contradict a clear biblical doctrine essential to the faith, such as whether Jesus is God. When dealing with digressions or unscriptural statements, the key is not to spend too much time on such items but to refocus the group. Never be afraid to correct a wrong statement, but always do it with kindness and respect. You may say, "That is an interesting thought, what do the rest of you think?" Then add in your thoughts that bring truth. If you believe what they said is wrong but don't know what is actually correct, be honest and say you would need to look into that. The goal is that no one thinks you are affirming an unbiblical thought that may confuse them.

A rabbit trail may include questions such as predestination, speaking in tongues, or any disputable doctrine. If you attempt to answer these topics, you may needlessly offend some, and the discussion will certainly take time away from the real issue at hand: how to become Proven Women. It's appropriate for you to stop the discussion by saying, "Let's refocus" or "Let's leave that topic for another day." If you find that you started or contributed to the conversation, admit that you opened the topic, but stress that you need to get back to the lesson for today. If it's an issue that someone says she really needs to address, ask her to contact the church leadership or another mature Christian woman outside of the group. If it's a matter that you believe must be addressed, such as whether a woman truly has become a Christian, you might tell her that you will talk to her later yourself. However, leave all disputable doctrines for another time and place. The point is that it's not necessary to dismiss the topic, but it is important to point out that there is not time to address it in this group.

When irrelevant topics do arise or the meetings turn into chit-chat, you need to become a good gatekeeper. Chances are that most side trips take you too far astray, so you will need to direct the group back to the lesson plan. Of course, you do want some spontaneous and open conversations, so it means you must weigh whether the discussion leads the women to grow from it.

SILENT PARTICIPANTS

There are two types of silence you must address: (1) the quiet person who rarely participates; and (2) the one who talks but does not openly share personal or vulnerable matters. You will need to gently prod the quiet woman. She likely will be easily steamrolled by others who are quick to speak or who act more forcefully. Therefore, you may need to say, "Laura, what do you think?" or "How about we hear from someone who has not spoken yet?" Allow there to be silence for a time. Remind the women that it is important for everyone to have the chance to participate.

With respect to those who do not share vulnerable details, begin by modeling it yourself. For example, tell the women you want to confess a lustful thought or an angry moment that you had this week. If you fail to show vulnerability and openness in discussing these topics or make it seem that you cannot identify with their struggles, some will be reluctant to openly share. Provide many opportunities for the women to share difficult things, and affirm them when they do. Regularly thank them for being open, and tell them that you love them and are proud of them. At times, it may be appropriate to give a woman a hug or place a gentle hand on her back, but don't use these gestures to stop or inhibit a good-flowing discussion. In addition, to help stimulate discussions regarding feelings, it is appropriate to ask the women personal questions, such as "Sara, how do you feel?" or "Brit, how did that make you feel?"

You may need to make a special effort to draw some women out. Look them in the eyes and engage with them directly. Keep asking them follow-up questions. At the end of each meeting, you should think if there were women who were withdrawn and how you could do better next time in opening them up and including them in the discussions.

There are many other types of communication problems that you will face when attitudes of pride or judgment surface. Be alert, and consider them to be opportunities for training.

Note about Sexual Abuse:

It's important to note that sexual abuse impacts the whole person—body, soul and spirit. The process of healing from the wounds of sexual abuse involves different stages and can look different for each woman. Statistics tell us that nearly one in every five women have experienced sexual abuse. Knowing all of this information, you need to be mindful of the fact that there may be women in your group who have experienced sexual abuse, and that an addiction to pornography and/or masturbation could have resulted from the abuse that they experienced. It's also important to note that a woman in your group may still be experiencing abuse.

While sharing stories in the first meeting some women may not feel comfortable sharing the fact that they have experienced abuse, while others may open up and share this freely with the group. Each woman who has experienced abuse will be in a different stage of healing, and because we may not know who is walking through this process, it's important that the topic of sexual abuse is mentioned in your first meeting.

The women in your group need to know that:

1. This is a safe space for them to be open about this topic (without going into detail that would be inappropriate for the group).

2. They are not alone.

3. The abuse they have experienced was not their fault.
4. They are capable of healing.

It is not your job to help them heal, but it is your job to point them toward Jesus, give them a safe space to learn, heal, and grow, and if possible, point them in the direction of professional help/counseling.

In the instructions for your first meeting there will be a section that references sexual abuse and an example of how to speak about this topic to your group.

As you prepare for your first group meeting, be sure to pray about this topic and seek the Lord for guidance.

Passionate for God,
Repentant in spirit,
Open and honest,
Victorious in living,
Eternal in perspective, and
Networking with other *Proven Women.*

# VII The Meetings

Plan to hold twelve to fourteen weekly meetings. You would need thirteen meetings to cover all twelve weeks in the *Study* because the first meeting consists of sharing stories and occurs prior to women starting the *Study*. It's important to plan in advance when to begin the session to ensure that you will end before a major holiday or vacation period where many women will not be able to attend.

The goal of each meeting is to put into practice the Proven elements to enter into a life that is devoted to the Lord and to develop healthy relationships. The first meeting should set the tone for the next twelve weeks and beyond. You will want to set the ground rules as well as alleviate any fears. Make it clear what is expected of the group members during the week, both while on their own and in the group meetings. Explain that it's important that the group not become a pity party and that there are particular points that need to be covered each week based upon the daily *Heartwork* assignments in the *Proven Study*. Let the group know that you may need to gently cut off some discussions and redirect others. Discuss how you expect each woman to participate but not to hog all of the time. Tell them that you will ask some to speak more often and others to speak less often, depending upon the way each woman communicates. Let them know that your comments are not personal and that you consider each woman to be a vital member of the team. Ask the women to accept, for now, that you will be the coach, having everyone's best interest in mind.

It's very important that you thoroughly prepare for each meeting. Begin by completing the daily *Heartwork* assignments each day during the week. You'll better relate to the women if you are working through the daily *Heartwork* assignments right along with them. Even if this means that you repeat the *Study* multiple times, it will show them your view of the importance of the materials and reinforce that

> You'll better relate to the women if you are working through the daily *Heartwork* assignments right along with them.

they, too, should redo the materials later. Besides, the Lord will meet with you in new and fresh ways each time you go through the *Study*.

In the week prior to each meeting, review the suggested outline for that week several times until you have a good idea of the framework on which you want to base the meeting. It may help you to jot down an outline, or you may want to write comments in the margins of the *Leader's Guide,* but in any case be prepared. Again, it's unlikely that you will be able to cover each point in the outline unless you monopolize each meeting and act as if you are merely teaching a class. Some items in the outline are crucial, and they will need to be stated in order for the women to receive certain training. Other items are designed to foster open communication with them. They need to start practicing vulnerability in a safe environment, and they may not communicate openly with a spouse or others outside of the group. Therefore, make sure each weekly group meeting contains opportunities to share in open and vulnerable ways. This is different from discussing a point of doctrine. You want the women to share deep personal matters that they would otherwise keep hidden behind thick walls. That's why it's a good idea to ask the women each week how they are feeling or what sexual struggles they have faced. Generally, each woman is allotted five minutes during this "check-in" time.

The twelve weeks will go fast, and it is likely that it will not be enough time for full healing to occur. In fact, healing often occurs during an entire lifetime. Group time is a great starting point, though, and it can be the doorway to a life committed to open relationships with God and others. A changed heart will continue to grow forever. That's why it's so important to foster a new and Proven lifestyle, complete with godly networking with other women. It can be a good idea to use the last night of the group to bring a sense of closure. Even though the last meeting will take place when there is still time left in the *Proven Study*, you might consider having a pizza party with a time of reflection and looking ahead. An outline for each meeting is attached in Appendix B. However, you have freedom to alter and adapt the meetings. Whatever schedule you end up following, though, it is important to include each of the elements needed for a Proven life in order to train women to center upon making intimacy with God and developing real relationships with others the top goals in life. In other words, don't cut out any of the six Proven elements, and guard against digressing into chit-chat or focusing too much time upon one woman's particular circumstances to the neglect of the others. Keep a healthy pursuit of the Lord as the primary mission of the women, because only when they meet with God will real change occur.

> Keep a healthy pursuit of the Lord as the primary mission of the women, because only when they meet with God will real change occur.

Things recommended to add to your meetings:

Prayer Partners: You can implement prayer partners in your group by dividing the women in your group into pairs. The reason for having prayer partners is to give each woman someone else to pray for and help keep accountable during the week. It's often extremely helpful in our journey to freedom to focus on the needs of others in our lives.

The goal of prayer partners is to meet in person or over phone or video once a week (separate from group meetings) to talk and pray with/for one another.

Take turns picking out the song for each week: Instead of picking the song for your group for worship each week, give each woman in your group a chance to pick out a song to worship to. Instruct them to choose a worship song and then after worship time has ended ask them to share with the group why they chose that specific song and how this particular song has impacted their relationship with the Lord.

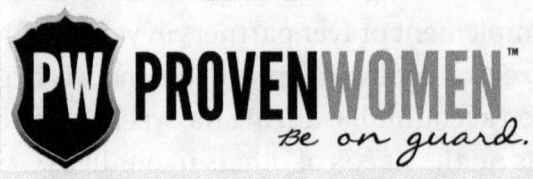

Passionate for God,
Repentant in spirit,
Open and honest,
Victorious in living,
Eternal in perspective, and
Networking with other *Proven Women.*

VIII. Helping Non-group Members

This type of group is closed, meaning that once you start, or at least after the second or third meeting, you will not add other members; yet you should expect women to approach you various times during the year when they cannot join the group. Even though they will not be able to attend your current group, there are several things you can do to help them outside of the group. First, be encouraging and demonstrate a longing for them to experience healing. Second, cover the materials from Week One, explaining the nature of sexual sin, the roots feeding it, and the cure. (See Appendix B.) Ask them to read the entire Proven website, www.ProvenWomen.org, as well as any other Proven books. After meeting with them and discussing the healing path, if they are willing to do whatever it takes to experience God's healing, then help them work out a plan. For instance, help them develop a daily quiet time that includes each of the elements of a Proven life, such as accountability. More specifically, encourage them to begin a life of daily prayer and study. Help them draw up an outline of a daily quiet time. This will vary for each woman, and the longer they are at it, the longer each woman will want to spend as she draws closer to the Lord. A good place to start is with quiet time that consists of: (1) praying for five minutes; (2) reading the New Testament and Psalms for five to ten minutes; (3) using a biblical study for fifteen minutes. You can even have them begin working through the *Study* on their own with weekly contact by you or another Proven woman. Alternatively, if there is a regular women's Bible study at your church, encourage them to attend it and to incorporate that study into their quiet times. In this way, they can begin networking with other Proven Women and start to pursue real, vulnerable relationships.

One of the most important things you should do is encourage them to develop and regularly meet with an accountability partner. Without that kind of weekly contact, in which they share their struggles and engage in open communications, they won't break free. That's just the way it works with most people. In addition, they may be so discouraged after incorrectly trying the "religious" route and still failing that they may even give up on the hope of experiencing

God's healing and decide not to join your next group. What they won't realize is that it was their faulty approach that missed the mark, not the lack of God's ability or desire to heal them.

To ensure that they link up with an accountability partner, you have several options to suggest, which include having you talk to them once a week by telephone or having you ask another sensitive and mature Christian woman to meet with them weekly. After holding a few Proven Women groups, you may notice that one or more women are particularly well suited to be accountability partners for these "in-between" women. In fact, if you have women that can never attend group because of scheduling conflicts, you could have someone who went through the Proven Women group redo the *Study* with that woman. She would act as an accountability partner and even meet weekly to discuss the *Study*. You could give this leader a copy of the *Leader's Guide* to aid her in ministering to the other woman while allowing her the freedom to alter the suggested outline to conform to a one-on-one meeting. You should regularly follow up with these women to strengthen and encourage them as well as to find out if they are growing or having problems that you can help address.

 # Life After Group

Because the goal of the group is to pursue an intimate relationship with God and walk in His purity and holiness, you need to encourage the women to transition to another Bible study at the end of one or more Proven small groups. The key is to encourage the women to start their next study immediately. If they relax or take a break from the pursuit of the Lord, then their hard-fought disciplines will evaporate. From the onset, you must foster the notion that healing is not a one-time event or a twelve-week program but consists of developing and maintaining a Proven lifestyle built upon real intimacy and relationships. If they understand and accept from the onset that this group is the first step and not a final solution, they will likely be more open to beginning the next study immediately. In addition, before the group ends, make sure each woman has her next study planned.

Because you will develop a closeness with the women in the group, you should plan on staying connected with each woman at some level of a relationship. Contact them periodically and ask about their walk with the Lord. Be a friend and encourager, not merely someone who wants to check up on them. Remember also, though, that you have earned the right to ask hard questions and to be as a blade of iron sharpening another blade of iron (Proverbs 27:17). Suggest that they also keep in contact with each other. Consider hosting a regular praise night, possibly quarterly or annually, where the women reunite to sing praise songs and connect. This can include a short time of sharing and a time of prayer. Eventually, it can even be broadened to include all of the former group members gathering for regular times of worship and prayer. Be creative in organizing events to stay connected, such as regular prayer walks or other activities.

Passionate for God,
Repentant in spirit,
Open and honest,
Victorious in living,
Eternal in perspective, and
Networking with other *Proven Women.*

Training Future Group Leaders

Although Christ loved all the same, He selected some to personally mentor and train to be leaders. You should seek out women who would make good leaders. When looking for someone to train to lead small groups, don't select a person solely based on her oral skills or what many people might think makes a good leader. Rather, pray for God to give you a woman after His own heart. The Lord wants women whose hearts are soft and devoted to Him. It's God's unconditional love that draws us to Him. Similarly, a gentle and kind woman with a large heart of mercy and compassion will be very useful to the Lord in being His instrument of healing in the lives of others.

The training process is quite simple. Spend lots of time with the woman you intend to train, such as inviting her and her family over for meals, going hiking, playing tennis, or establishing a regular time of talking. Include her in discussions about your goals and dreams. Talk to her about how to minister to others who struggle. Allow the spark to become a roaring fire as you both long to be servants of the Lord. As you talk to her, discuss personal matters as well as hobbies, struggles, and victories. One of the best ways to solidify a bond is to establish a weekly time of prayer together. For instance, you could meet at 6:30 in the morning to walk in the park together to pray for thirty minutes or pray on the telephone together. You could also meet with her at other scheduled prayer events or meetings at church. If your church does not have a weekly prayer group you can attend, then start one. The church would likely allow you to use a room each week to begin a prayer meeting.

At some point, ask the person you are mentoring to lead a small group. Depending upon the person, she could co-lead with you or begin leading on her own right away. If you ask her to co-lead, decide who will be the primary leader so that there are no misunderstandings or anxiety over the uncertainty of her role. If you provide sufficient guidance, she could lead a group with or without you being present. For some, it might be best if you don't attend the group. They would do better not worrying about each thing they say. For instance, if you are

Proven Women: The Leader's Guide

at the meeting, the woman you have mentored might constantly turn to you and ask if what she just explained was correct. Her attention may be more focused on pleasing you or performing for you than upon the task at hand.

XI. Using These Materials for Regular Women's Groups

It's not necessary to create a formal recovery group to host a study based upon these materials. The *Proven Study* makes a great group Bible study for women's groups. It can be less intimidating for some to use these materials during an ongoing women's group. Simply use the *Proven Study* as the next study aid.

There is no reason that any women's ministry at any church could not use the *Proven Study* as a Bible study, regardless of the size of the group. The leader merely needs to generate a few probing questions, facilitate discussion, and, most importantly, allow open sharing. The questions can be as simple as asking what struck the women from the materials and what principles they learned, as well as asking them to openly share struggles, hope, or victory they experience during each week. You can even have the women find specific accountability partners and have each pair call one other once during the week to pray and ask if they have any struggles or need any encouragement.

Passionate for God,
Repentant in spirit,
Open and honest,
Victorious in living,
Eternal in perspective, and
Networking with other *Proven Women.*

Conclusion

You are capable of forming and leading small groups, because the Holy Spirit is your guide. However, never lose focus that your goal is to meet with the Lord daily and to seek Him with all of your heart. Even though we all are made to minister to others, you are not responsible for anyone's healing. Above all, don't lose your personal relationship with the Lord in attempts to serve Him. Keep putting the elements of a Proven life into practice daily, and the Lord will guide your path. If God wants you to run a group, there is no power on earth that will prevent it from happening in His timing. Conversely, if you act outside of His will and timing, or if you allow pride to be a driving force, no amount of good leadership skills will make your group flourish. Remember that an intimate prayer life will move God into action and open the hearts of the women He wants you to lead to Him for healing and true intimacy.

FINAL REMARKS

We are so excited that you are considering leading a small group, and we anticipate hearing from you. Please contact us (stay connected) and give us reports so that we can share in your joy as a single team of godly women striving for absolute purity and reaching for divine union with our dear Lord and Creator. Send us an email at info@ProvenMen.org.

A FEW FINAL ADMONITIONS

- Enjoy God, minister to your family, and do the things you have learned and will learn.
- Keep praying for and fellowshipping with your sisters in Christ.
- Know that you are dearly loved and are God's most treasured possession!
- Keep finding meaningful and pleasing ways to worship your precious Lord.
- Continue each day in study, in God's Word, and in prayer. Make sure you begin your next study immediately.

PERSONAL SALUTATION FROM THE FOUNDER OF PROVEN MEN MINISTRIES, LTD.

I have no greater joy than to hear that fellow Proven Men and Women are walking victoriously in the truth. Please make my joy complete by being like-minded, having the same love and passion for the Lord and each other, and becoming one in spirit and purpose. I look forward to reading emails and testimonies from you and witnessing the work of the Lord through your life and in the lives of those you touch.

Go forth. Live a holy and pure life embracing the Proven Latin battle cry, *Coram Deo*, "Before the eyes of the Lord!" By presenting yourself to God as an approved worker, you will no longer need to be ashamed but will correctly handle the word of truth, which God entrusts to you, His friend (see 2 Timothy 2:15). Keep referring to the *PROVEN* acronym to remind yourself how to live and whom to live for!

Passionate for God,

Repentant in spirit,

Open and honest,

Victorious in living,

Eternal in perspective, and

Networking with other **Proven Women.**

 # Appendix A: Sample Ground Rules

1. Maintaining Strict Confidentiality. What is shared in the group stays in the group. I will not disclose what others share in the group, and I will not reveal the names of group members. If I ever violate this confidence, I will humbly confess it and seek forgiveness.

2. Taking Responsibility for My Own Actions. I understand that healing is a process with a purpose and that I am responsible for seeking and receiving healing from the Lord. Therefore, I will commit to making it a high priority to use the *Proven Study* each day in meeting with the Lord, who alone can heal and change me. I will humbly and willingly cooperate with God and rely upon His strength to overcome.

3. Attending Group. I realize that my attendance at each group meeting is important for myself as well as to the other group members. Therefore, I commit to making each meeting a high priority. I will rearrange my schedule to avoid conflicts, and I will attend meetings even when I am tired or do not feel like it. If I simply cannot make a meeting, I will notify the group leader in advance. In addition, I will make it a point to attend on time. If I ever arrive late, I will slip in quietly and will not disrupt the meeting by announcing my presence or by greeting others.

4. Participating in Meetings. I will work hard at recognizing and sharing my feelings. I will also work through difficulties and actively participate in discussions in an open, real, and vulnerable manner. In addition, I will guard against bringing up side issues, arguing over disputable doctrines, or raising other matters that take away from an atmosphere where all are encouraged to share difficult personal issues and to work toward a healing path. If the leader informs me that I have gotten off topic, I will not argue with her but will give her grace in leading the discussions.

5. Respecting Others. I will show respect to all group members. For instance, I will be mindful of any tendency I may have to dominate conversations or to monopolize sharing times in order that others have at least the same amount of time to share. When others are speaking, I will give them my undivided attention, and I will not interrupt them or try to solve their problems. In addition, I will not judge another group member or compare myself to her. Finally, I will pray for each woman throughout the week.

6. Keeping Evil Out. The group is to be a safe place. Therefore, I will not bring into the meetings things that may cause my sisters to stumble. For instance, I will refrain from discussing unnecessary graphic details about sexual matters, which might be a trigger for another person. However, I will not use this ground rule as a means of avoiding being open and honest in personal sharing, including making appropriate confession of sexual sins. Finally, if I experience a setback or struggle just before a group meeting, I will not use this rule as a reason for skipping a meeting or as a way of sabotaging my healing.

Appendix B: Detailed Leader's Guides for All Group Meetings

Attached is a very detailed outline for thirteen weekly small group meetings. Each weekly outline has more than enough material and discussion questions to fill a two-hour meeting. Be flexible and don't expect to be able to get through all of the items on a given day. Instead, be ready to tailor the material to your group so that you can cover the most pertinent and beneficial information during each group meeting.

As a group leader, you have freedom to follow the suggested outline or to modify it to meet your group dynamics and personal style of relating. For instance, it is detailed enough to position a woman who has never led a group to effectively lead one, yet it is also designed to provide structure and sufficient *Heartwork* discussions for seasoned small group leaders. All of the scriptural truths and spiritual insights in this guide are useful for the group meetings and are intended to be shared with the group, but it's important to note that this outline is not intended to be a script. Each group of women will have personal and specific needs, and the material used in the group meetings can be adapted to suit a particular group. For this reason, it's imperative that as the leader, you remain open to the leading of the Holy Spirit and attentive to God's voice as you conduct each weekly meeting. For that reason, we have included *Leader's Notes* that are indented and a different font to set them apart. They are suggestions for comments you can make or additional discussion topics or questions. Feel free to use, ignore or modify them.

Some groups prefer to end with a song rather than begin with a song. Other groups always begin by asking what items from the daily *Study* impacted each person. Feel free to modify this *Leader's Guide*, but be sure that you read through the *Leader's Guide* before each group meeting to gain any insights and to plan out your meeting with a level of detail. This will help keep the meetings from turning into long discussions about daily work events and home life rather than a time to engage with the Lord in addressing the root issues that keep women in bondage to sin.

Proven Women: The Leader's Guide

Don't forget that the first meeting centers around sharing stories and establishing group dynamics. The second meeting discusses the first week of the companion *Proven Study* materials.

You also need to have the women purchase a *Study* prior to the first meeting so she can begin right away without any delay. (You might consider purchasing a few extra *Studies* to have available.)

The next page begins with the Week One meeting.

WEEK 1

REMINDERS

The first week could be longer than future meetings, depending on how many ladies are in your group. When you invite women to attend, let them know that the first meeting will last between two and three hours, but future meetings will not go past two hours. This is because each woman will be sharing her story and there is much to cover.

Plan to read through the following suggested meeting guide several times in order to become comfortable with the material. You should also reread it just before the meeting. Bring the *Leader's Guide* with you and any other notes you made for holding the meeting. Be sure each woman has a copy of the *Study* prior to the first meeting or plan to purchase enough copies of the *Study* for each woman.

GOALS FOR THIS FIRST GROUP MEETING

1. Making the group a place of security where each woman can be open and honest.
2. Setting the expectations and tone for the group
3. Training women to meet with God and receive His healing.

The group will only be as vulnerable in openness and sharing or as devoted to prayer as you show yourself to be. Your role is to lead by example. If you are reserved with visible walls, the women will model that behavior as well! In this first meeting, you will set the tone for the entire group.

OPENING PRAYER

After spending some time greeting one another, open with prayer. Remember, prayer is not just a way to open a group, but it is a time of dedicating this group session to the Lord. It is a time of inviting Him into the group and letting His Spirit lead the discussion.

SINGING

Sing one song at the beginning (or end) of each meeting. We are striving to cultivate a heart of worship, and setting aside time specifically to worship God will be a great habit to develop during this study. Remind the ladies that the purpose of this time is to be mindful of who God is, to exalt His name, or quiet their heart before Him.

> Always reserve three to five minutes in each group meeting for singing a song. It is acceptable to place singing either as the first element after opening prayer or to include it at the end just before closing prayer. Having the singing time immediately after the opening prayer is most common and can really set the stage for the meetings. The easiest way to have music for the meetings is to play it from your phone or mobile speaker. It is vital that you bring the words to the song. If you play the music loudly enough, and have a printout of the words for each woman, everyone will join in. Begin the first night with a song you think fits the mood you are establishing, namely the hope found in Christ through yielding entirely to Him and living out a Proven life. Remember, though, that you must select songs that are singable, not just a favorite trendy song.

DISCUSSION/TEACHING

GROUND RULES

> Prior to the meeting, consider copying the ground rules attached as Appendix A and hand out copies at the meeting. Recap the main points and ask if there are any questions. It is vital that your group takes ownership of these ground rules. Ask them if there are any rules which they want to add. Ask if they are willing to accept each of these rules and hold one another accountable to them.
>
> As the leader, plan on doing the *Study* each day yourself. Tell your group that you are committing to doing the *Study* every day, and ask them to make the same commitment.

Detailed Leader's Guides for All Group Meetings: Week One

WORD PICTURES (OPTIONAL)

Just as people don't starve for a week and then eat one big meal, it is vital that each woman plans to do the *Study* each day rather than attempting to do multiple days' worth right before the group meets. However, it is important that they know they shouldn't be discouraged if they cannot complete every item. The *Study* is very intensive, and some won't be able to get through every item each day; that is okay. The key point is to commit to meeting with the Lord daily with the purpose of getting to know Him. In fact, these materials won't change anyone; only God can do that, so each woman must plan on meeting with God daily.

SHARING YOUR STORY

Share your story...

> Your story should be five to ten minutes. The length you speak sets the stage for the rest of the ladies. If you only share a couple minutes, they will do the same and possibly not share as much as they need to. But you don't want to go too long so that there is plenty of time for the rest of the group. Be sure to include enough details about your struggles so that they can identify and feel comfortable sharing similar details. Also, let them know that you are now walking in victory. The goal is not to brag, but to show hope. Everyone's history is a little bit different, but your story may start like this: "Let me begin by sharing a little about my own story. The funny thing about my story is that I once made an oath to myself never to tell another person that I masturbated. I was going to go to the grave with that secret. But God changed my heart and freed me from guilt and shame. Here is how it all started for me."
>
> With your story, share how it started, how God began the process of healing for you, and where you are now. Be sure to make this about God's victory in your life and not your own effort or victory.

After you have shared, tell them:
- Ladies, I have just shared my story. Some of you may have similar struggles as me and some may be very different. The beauty of the gospel is that no sin is too big, too dark, or too deep for God to cleanse and forgive. There is such freedom in admitting these struggles out loud, bringing the darkness to the light. As you share your story, I want to encourage you to be as specific as you need to be. Don't be afraid to use the words pornography, masturbation, same-sex attraction, affairs, sex, fantasies. You don't need to share any details of content that you have watched or done, but be specific with whether you struggle with watching or reading or imagining or being physical with another person.

Proven Women: The Leader's Guide

We want to get these things out in the open so that Satan no longer has power over them as hidden sins.

LISTENING TO THEIR STORIES

Next, invite the women to share their stories, how they got to where they are, and where they want to be. Give each woman five to ten minutes. *If someone begins to cry as she is sharing, don't try to stop her from crying. Tell her it's okay to cry and give her permission to cry out as much as she needs to. Tears can be very cleansing and healing.*

Each time a woman shares, be sure to affirm her. Thank her for being open and tell her you are proud of her for sharing.

There may be a need to ask a few questions if it was not clear in a particular woman's story as to where she is in her personal struggle. You might need to ask, "Can I ask some short questions to allow me to understand better where you are at right now?"

Some possible questions include:
- *When was the last time you masturbated? How often?*
- *When did you last look at or read pornography? How often?*
- *What sexual sin is the biggest struggle that you now face?*

*Remember to be very sensitive and affirming about God's grace and forgiveness toward their sin.

After everyone has shared, tell them:
- There is freedom in confession of sins. 1 John 1:9 says, "If we confess our sins, He is faithful and just to forgive us and cleanse us of all unrighteousness." I hope you experience that freedom. We have to accept that forgiveness with faith. For me, I have no more secrets, unconfessed sins, and therefore, Satan has no hold on me. If any unconfessed sins come to your mind, feel free to share them now. God wants to give you freedom. God is faithful to forgive each sin that we confess, so be sure to confess each one to Him. It may be impossible to recount every sexual sin, but if anything else comes to mind now or later, you have the freedom to share it, okay?

Feel free to state this in your own words.

Detailed Leader's Guide for All Group Meetings: Week One

Say:

Before we move forward with the rest of tonight's meeting, I also wanted to mention something important.

Some of you in this group may have experienced sexual abuse in your past or may even still be experiencing it now. I want you to know that this is a safe space to share, ask for prayer, and ask for help.

As you go through this study, memories and thoughts about past abuse may come up in your mind. You may realize that some of the unhealthy habits or addictions you're facing have stemmed from the abuse you've endured. When these thoughts surface, I want you to remember a few important things:

1. The abuse you've endured was not your fault. Any guilt that you may feel is FALSE. You are not responsible for the actions of someone else. You did nothing to deserve the abuse you've experienced.

2. You are not alone. Satan likes to make us feel isolated and alone, but this is just a lie that he wants us to believe.

3. You can't control what has happened to you, but you can take control of how you will choose to react now. Just being a part of this group is a great start to the healing process.

4. Healing is possible, and there is nothing that Jesus cannot help you overcome!

In chapter 6 of the *Study*, we will touch on the topic of abuse and forgiveness as a group. As you go through the *Study* remember these four important things and that you are never alone in all of this.

HOW DOES GOD SEE US?

Say:

We have all gone around and confessed many things that we have done wrong. The question that we have to ask ourselves now is how do we think God sees us in view of all of these things? If we could make eye contact with God right now, what do we think we would see in His eyes? Love? Delight? Anger? Disappointment? Frustration?

The truth is, what you ***think*** you would see in His eyes will dictate whether you would go to Him or not. If you think you will be met with frustration or disappointment, it is so much easier to just avoid God.

It is so important for us to actually KNOW God's view of us and not just base it on our feelings.

Read this story to the ladies:

It is very important for us to understand how the gospel affects God's view of us. Let me share Hannah's story with you. Hannah grew up in a Christian family and understood the gospel and how it brings eternal life. She had given her heart to Jesus when she was in junior high and knew she would go to heaven someday. As she got older, she got caught up in the party scene. She wanted to be accepted by her peers and so she joined the crowd. She knew she shouldn't be doing this, but she really didn't think it was that big of a deal. Pornography eventually made its way into her life. After a while, however, the pornography was not enough, and she eventually began having sex with the guys in her life. By the time Emily met Hannah, she had finally rid herself of the party and porn scene but was having a very hard time saying no to sexual sin.

Hannah said she enjoyed the physical part of a relationship—talking to that person, making eye contact, being with them. And since she couldn't do that with God, she turned to guys to feel loved and eventually that turned into sexual sin. Emily asked her a few questions.

Emily asked: Hannah, how do you think God views you right now? Don't give me the Sunday school answer, I want to know what your gut tells you.

Hannah said: I know he is disappointed in me and He probably thinks that He wasted His breath on me when He made me.

Emily asked: Why do you think that, Hannah?

Hannah said: I try so hard to be the person that I am supposed to be. But it seems like I can never be that person, and no matter how hard I try, I fail. Knowing that I am not enough to please God makes me give up trying and go back to something that does make me feel valuable. Sex makes me feel valued.

Ask:
- How about us? How do we think God views us? What does our gut tell us about God's perspective of us?

    Let the ladies go around and share their answers.

Continue Reading:

Back to Hannah's story: At this point, Emily walked Hannah through the gospel. It is true, we all fall short. We are all broken, sinful people, and no matter how hard we try, we will never be enough. We will never arrive. We will always fall short. We fell short before we put our faith in Jesus, but we also fall short every day after we put our faith in Jesus. God knew that. Yet He desired a relationship with us so He had Christ die on the cross to take on every single bit of our sin—past, present, and future. On our best day, we fall short, yet Christ covers us, and it is through Christ that we get access to God. On our worst day, we fall short, yet God loves us too much to push us away; so on our worst day, Christ grants us access to God if we are willing to come to Him in humility. We do not have to fear condemnation in God's eyes. He looks on us with love, acceptance, and favor because we come with Christ. We get the welcome that Jesus deserves.

God humbled himself by becoming a man, Jesus the Son of God. He went to the cross on behalf of Hannah and took on all of the shame and wrath of her sexual sin so that she would be free of the shame. Hannah is clothed in Jesus' righteousness, so she is forgiven and granted access to her heavenly Father in her time of need. Jesus conquered death on the cross by rising from the dead. Her shame is no more. Because of the cross, God never turns His back on Hannah even in the midst of her sin. He stands with arms open wide always ready to receive Hannah. But for her to walk into God's arms, she must be willing to turn from her sin and turn toward God. She cannot face God and sin at the same time because they are in opposite directions. To return to the Father, she must repent, turn away from the sin and acknowledge God. But she never has to fear His dismay, His condemnation, or His disappointment. Not because she does not deserve those things. Nor because God has decided those things are okay and she is not accountable for them. He already cast all of those things onto Jesus. God didn't hold back. Jesus had to pay them in full for Hannah. And he paid them in full for you.

After Emily explained all of this to Hannah, Hannah assured Emily that she had gotten saved in junior high; however, she had not understood how the gospel freed her from her current sin and shame. She truly thought that God was so mad at her and that she couldn't fight her way back into his love and favor.

So, Emily asked Hannah again…

Emily: Hannah, how does God see you?

Hannah said (with new awe in her voice): He saved me!!

Emily asked: Why did he save you, Hannah?

Hannah said: Because he loves me! (Seriously, the only word that can describe her voice is incredulous. She finally believed it yet couldn't believe it was true. She finally understood amazing grace!)

Emily asked: What did He save you from?

Hannah said: All of my sin. Even this sin I just told you about.

Then Hannah went on to discover that the reason she didn't go to God was not because she couldn't have a physical conversation with Him, but because she always feared His rejection. Once she realized she would always be welcomed and accepted by Him, she knew she was valued and no longer needed the sexual relationships with guys to feel like she was enough.

The truth is, Satan is the accuser, and he wants us to believe that God is disgusted with us and will only welcome us when we are walking in righteousness. But this is not the gospel. Romans 8:1 "There is therefore no condemnation for those who are in Christ Jesus." When we turn to God with reverence and humility, we can trust that God is looking at us with loving eyes that are free of condemnation. He is not angry. He is not disgusted. His kindness is meant to bring us to repentance. And our repentance allows Him to forgive and cleanse us from all unrighteousness (I John 1:9). The only way to freedom is by being with the Father. But in order to be willing to go to the Father, we need to be sure of what His response to us will be.

THE PRODIGAL SON

Read Luke 15:11-32.

Ask:
- What stands out about the Father in this story?
- What did the son have to do in order to be welcomed by the Father?

State:
- This story is more about the Father than it is about the prodigal son. The son went away in order to live for himself in sin. He dishonored the Father, yet the Father was waiting for his return. As soon as the Father saw the son coming His way, the Father closed the distance and welcomed the son. Do we trust that this will be God's response when we turn from our sin and return to Him? Do we expect to be welcomed back, or do we think we have to work to gain favor again? Unless we believe in the Father's love and forgiveness, we will always feel the need to hide from God until we are better with our sin. We will never be better apart from receiving help from the Father.

Detailed Leader's Guides for All Group Meetings: Week One

COMMITMENT TIME

Ask:
- Is this something you want? Will you agree to give God total and complete control of your life, including your hands, heart, and mind? Will you agree to run to God in your moment of temptation or sin?

  It may be useful to go around the room and let each of the women answer individually. If any say no or that they are not sure, ask them and then discuss what is holding them back. Do not pressure an answer. God's timing is perfect, and it must be a work of the Holy Spirit in order to be lasting. Remind the women of God's promise: If anyone is willing to do whatever it takes to be free from sin and to pursue the Lord, then she will experience freedom. God promises to give His power to those who submit to him fully, and they can overcome.

PROVEN WOMEN SMALL GROUPS

Continue:
- Let me tell you how the Proven Women small group fits into this picture. The goal and purpose of the weekly groups is not to cure you of a sickness, and it is not a program for stopping lust. Instead, it is intended to position you to meet with God and to receive His power by learning how to turn the focus off yourself and onto God. You will practice living to love God. It is sometimes called daily *Heartwork* because it is designed to make your heart change as it meets with God each day. The *Study* requires a lot of effort, but in the end you will be renewed and will know God. Your actions will be holy as He is holy.

  Feel free to state this in your own words.

REINFORCING WHAT THE LETTERS *PROVEN* REPRESENT

State:
- Here is the meaning behind the letters *PROVEN* and how important it is for each and every element to be incorporated into your daily lives:

  P is for Passionate for God,

  R is for Repentant in spirit,

  O is for Open and honest,

  V is for Victorious in living,

E is for Eternal in perspective, and

N is for Networking with other **Proven Women.**

State:
- Remember what the *PROVEN* acronym stands for and to test your life daily against each element. A PROVEN woman is **P**assionately following God. She recognizes that she has sin in her heart and **R**epents to God, bowing in humility before him. She is **O**pen and honest to herself, God, and trusted friends. In fact, as she learns to trust God even more, she is willing to dig a little deeper into her heart, not fearing what is below the surface. If it is sinful, God will cleanse it and forgive it. If it is painful, God will bring comforting love and care while healing it. She begins to see **V**ictory and her choices, celebrating those victories with God who she recognizes is right beside her and powering every step. As she grows closer with God, she is often reminded to have an **E**ternal perspective. She loves God so much that she cannot wait for the day she will know him fully when she sees him face-to-face. Yet while here on this earth, she knows she has purpose as she continues to grow to know God more and make him known to others. She **N**etworks with other women who continue to encourage her and hold her up while she is weak, and she also gets to encourage other women who are on this journey with Christ. She is PROVEN yet she is human. She will mess up. She will be disappointed, and experience trials and hardships. At times life will be mundane and boring. There will be times she wants to throw in the towel. But Christ will be with her to encourage her, comfort her, strengthen her, refine her, and pick her back up. She never has to do this alone. And if she forgets that and tries to do it alone, he will come alongside her and remind her.

State:
- In your daily *Study* and during group, you will learn how to live out a Proven life in which your focus and desires shift. In short, it is a place to grow in newness of life and to experience lasting healing in all areas of your life as you yield yourself to the One who created you and loves you. Sure, you'll still face temptations and trials in life, but you will rest in God's power to overcome, and you'll enjoy real relationships instead of the false intimacy, which produces guilt and shame and never satisfies.

   Feel free to state this in your own words.

Ask:
- Do you have any questions?

Detailed Leader's Guides for All Group Meetings: Week One

CLOSING PRAYER

Reserve the last ten to fifteen minutes for prayer.

> Be a role model in your prayers. God does not delight in fine-sounding words, but rather a heart that is open to Him and longing to meet with Him. Passion and repentance are hallmarks of humility, which please the Lord and lead to transformation. Give each woman an opportunity to pray by taking turns going around the room. You should begin with a short prayer, pouring out your heart and seeking absolute purity in your life. Go around the room, allowing each woman to pour out her heart in prayer. Tell them that God wants our hearts, not our fancy words, so we should talk to Him from our hearts.

Before they leave, **ask each woman to write down her telephone number and email address** so that you can contact them.

> Expect that the other women might want to exchange these things as well. Even the thought that you will contact them during the week can add strength. Never forget that the battles will be fierce for the women. Your loving, caring contact can mean a lot. You don't need to ask them each time you talk to them outside of group if they stumble. Rather, be encouraging. Tell them that you just wanted to call and see how they are doing and whether there is anything you can pray about with them. Conversely, if you don't have regular contact, Satan will bring thoughts into their heads that you don't care or will otherwise seek to tempt them into reverting to coping mechanisms.

Tell the women to bring their *Study* guide and a Bible to each group.

Give each woman a hug as you say good-bye.

> If you keep this consistent, you won't have to keep reminding them to hug each other at the start and end of each meeting.

HOMEWORK

Tell the women to pray for each other during the week, do the first week of the *Study,* and return to group next week. Each week you will be discussing the previous week's material.

SELF-CRITIQUE OF MEETING

After each weekly session, you should conduct a self-evaluation of the meeting. If you have a co-leader, plan to spend ten minutes talking after the group or the next day. Some questions to ponder are:

- *Overall, how would I rate the meeting?*
- *Was there anything I would change or do differently next time?*
- *Was I open and honest, being vulnerable and caring?*
- *Did I spend too much time talking or teaching?*
- *Did I ask questions that drew the women out and did I allow them to respond?*
- *Did each woman have enough opportunity to share?*
- *Was there anyone who was closed off or talked only at a surface level?*
- *Is there a woman I need to call to check on this week?*
- *How well did I manage the time?*
- *Did we have enough time for singing and prayer?*

Be honest in your appraisal. It is important that you create an environment that is not only safe but is also a place to openly share. It is very important to assess each meeting so that your preparation for the next is even better. For instance, if you find that you are talking too much, write out some questions that invite others to share. If, on the other hand, the meetings tend to be more chit-chat sessions about how family is doing or what activities each person did during the week, then prepare a more detailed outline that reduces time spent talking about events of the day.

PREPARATION FOR NEXT WEEK

Be sure to establish some form of contact with the women each week. Be fully prepared for the meetings. Review your notes from the *Study*, which you should do at the same time as the others in the group, even if it means you go through the *Study* more than once a year. Write out an outline or make notes in the margins of this guide.

SEND A TEXT TO THE WOMEN

Note: Each week send an encouraging email or text to the women. A sample is provided for each week. Feel free to send it or create your own. Following is a suggestion:

I enjoyed meeting with you this week. I am excited to be part of your life and watching you grow. I am here for you. I am praying for you. Please call me anytime you need to talk or just want me to pray with you. Keep at it. I believe in you.

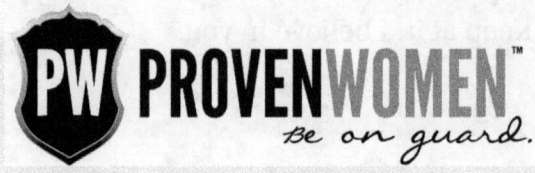

Passionate for God,
Repentant in spirit,
Open and honest,
Victorious in living,
Eternal in perspective, and
Networking with other *Proven Women.*

MEMORY VERSE

Romans 8:1 "'There is therefore now no condemnation for those who are in Christ Jesus."

WEEK  (based on Week One *Study* materials)

This week is based on Week One of the *Study*. Be sure to start a practice of hugging each woman as you greet them before the meeting, and ask the others to do the same.

We are striving to cultivate healthy intimacy among the group.

OPENING PRAYER

After spending some time greeting one another, open with prayer. Remember, prayer is not just a way to open your group, but also a time of dedicating this group session to the Lord, inviting Him into the conversation, and letting His Spirit lead the discussion.

SINGING

Each week be prepared to listen to a song. This can either be for everyone to listen and meditate or to sing along together as a group. Encourage the ladies to look up the lyrics on their phones in order to sing along or have a handout.

CHECK-IN

State:
- Turn to the *Feelings Chart* in Appendix F of the companion *Study*. I want each of you to spend five minutes describing your feelings now, how you felt during the week, and how your week went. It's good to be honest with our feelings. Rather than bury feelings, we need to bring them before the Lord. If they are painful, He will comfort. If they are ugly,

such as selfish or jealous, then through confessing them, He will forgive and cleanse. We work through our emotions by bringing them before the Lord in honest admission.

> Make sure each woman shares. Plan to include a check-in time every meeting. The women need to practice knowing and openly sharing their feelings. For some ladies, being able to identify and name their emotions will bring such clarity to their life. Oftentimes we get emotional and overwhelmed and just jumble our emotions together. It is important to be able to articulate how we are feeling.

> Consider telling the women that men are often known for not having feelings and women are often known for being too emotional. The truth is, we all have feelings and we need to be able to identify and express them. This is a crucial aspect of being in healthy relationships with others.

GOD STORIES and CONFESSION

State the next three paragraphs in your own words:

It is important to recognize that a lot can happen in a week. Each of us could experience both devastating setbacks as well as tremendous victory within a week's time. Each week, we will set aside a time for both confession as well as God stories.

This should be a safe place where it is expected that we confess any setbacks from the previous week. There are some very good reasons to confess setbacks:

1. God says that if we confess our sins, He is faithful to forgive (1 John 1:9). That means that each time we confess we can be assured that forgiveness from Him will follow.
2. When we confess our sins and share our struggles with each other a weight is lifted off our chests. We no longer have to hide anything anymore, and shame that we've felt will start to fade away (James 5:16).
3. When we share our struggles and setbacks we no longer have any secrets, and this is how we begin to free ourselves from the hold that Satan tries to have on us. Satan wants us to keep holding secrets and live in fear of being found out. That's how he likes to control us and keep us from living the lives that Christ has planned for us. Many women go through life with the fear that if people really knew them, they wouldn't like them. They are always afraid of being found out, so they close their hearts to others. When we choose vulnerability we break that pattern.

Each week, it is also great to share victories or God stories. When we only focus on the failures, we can get discouraged. God is always at work around us, and we need to be training ourselves to be looking for how He is working in our lives. It could be that He gave someone the strength to overcome a temptation. It could be that they saw the way of escape during a temptation (1 Corinthians 10:13), whether or not they took it. Plan to spend time each week celebrating each of our God stories as well.

State:

Ladies, now we are going to go around and share how our weeks went. This will be a time of both confession as well as God stories. Let's praise God for how He has worked in our lives this week. Let's also confess where we fell short. But remember, even in the ways we fell short, let's praise God for His grace and forgiveness.

> *If a woman confesses that she looked at pornography or masturbated, thank her for being open. Without sounding judgmental, consider asking follow-up questions, such as, "What led up to that?" and "What did you do afterward?" Be sure to affirm her, thanking her for being open and telling her you love her.*

> *When someone confesses a sin, make sure to respond in an affirming way, reminding them that this sin does not define them and that God is very willing to forgive and cleanse. Then ask if they have already confessed it before the Lord. Always give the woman an opportunity to pray right then, confessing it before the Lord and thanking God for His forgiveness if she hasn't already done so. It is important that this woman pray herself rather than someone praying for her. She needs to be willing to take responsibility and ownership of her sin before the Lord. Obviously, if she is not willing to pray herself, others can pray for her, but she needs to understand that bringing these before the Lord is a great goal for her to have.*

> *Always encourage them to also share God stories.*

ACTION PLAN

After you have given everyone an opportunity to speak tell them:

Thank you all for sharing, I very much appreciate your authenticity. I am grateful you are willing to trust us enough to confess in this group. Let's also remember that we have the ability to confess to God throughout the week and that we don't have to wait for the group. Each time we sin, it's important to turn immediately to the Lord. God forgives us when we ask. We don't have to wait until we feel like we deserve forgiveness; it is by God's perfect grace that we receive it.

State:

Once we confess, we need to have a game plan of turning away from sin. Here is an example: When you take a second look or have a lustful thought, tell God right away, repent and ask for forgiveness. Once you do, immediately accept God's grace and forgiveness. Then turn to praise or other godly activity, such as reading a verse or praying for someone you know. Turning to a godly activity is a great reminder that your sin didn't disqualify you from meeting with God. It is important for us to first repent, but in that moment, we are forgiven and free to sprint to God. Your heart is free to worship Him and give thanks!

MEMORY VERSE

***Ask someone to recite the memory verse, Romans 8:1, or ask someone to read it aloud from the* Study.**

Ask:

Describe what the verse means, and how you think it fits into a healing path.

> Be ready to discuss how it is so important to realize that because of Christ's death and resurrection on the cross, we no longer walk in condemnation. It is vital for us to realize that we have the freedom to come to Christ without fear of condemnation. I believe that shame makes people hide from God, and that is the number one thing that keeps people in their sin. We have to really combat the mentality that we do not deserve to go to God in this moment. Without the gospel, that would be a true statement, but that is the very thing the gospel accomplished. Christ came to close the gap between God and us, even in our worst moments.

State:
- Grace does not give us the freedom to continue in sin, but grace does give us the freedom to be completely honest about our current sin without fear of condemnation. You should have read and meditated on this sentence this week. What has this truth meant to you?

> Give time for responses.

DISCUSSION/TEACHING

GOD AS CREATOR

Read through the lesson and share it in your own words.

The *Study* began by walking us through the gospel, and the gospel begins with God as Creator. As we move through the weeks ahead, it is vital that we know who God is. God is the Creator who designed life. He knows what is good and life-giving. He knows what is evil and destructive. God loves immeasurably more than we can imagine. Anything that He calls good is for our good and for His glory. Anything He calls evil is destructive to our well-being and also moves us away from Him.

Although God created everything good, because of the fall, we are broken.

Thankfully, because of Christ, we can be restored.

Do we trust that God's way is best? Why or why not?

> Let this be a very honest discussion. We may be very quick to think, "Absolutely, I believe God's way is best." But then, when we look at our thoughts or our actions, we realize that we have a tendency to question God and His design. Some may think God is stuffy and old-fashioned and does not want anyone to have fun. Some may think God is not fair. The truth is, God created all that is good, including adventure, fun, life, laughter, love, joy, sex, and intimacy.

Since God is the Designer, we must trust He knows best. His infinite wisdom weighs in so much stronger than our own limited perspective. Also, His knowledge is based on truth, love, and goodness while ours is often tainted.

Read Psalm 19:7-11
The law of the Lord is perfect,[c]
   reviving the soul;
the testimony of the Lord is sure,
   making wise the simple;
[8] the precepts of the Lord are right,
   rejoicing the heart;
the commandment of the Lord is pure,
   enlightening the eyes;
[9] the fear of the Lord is clean,
   enduring forever;
the rules[d] of the Lord are true,
   and righteous altogether.
[10] More to be desired are they than gold,
   even much fine gold;
sweeter also than honey
   and drippings of the honeycomb.
[11] Moreover, by them is your servant warned;
   in keeping them there is great reward.

Proven Women: The Leader's Guide

Read 2 Timothy 3:16-17

"[16] All Scripture is breathed out by God and profitable for teaching, for reproof, for correction, and for training in righteousness, [17] that the man of God[b] may be complete, equipped for every good work."

Ask:

What do these passages say about the Bible?

Read Isaiah 55:8-9 "For my thoughts are not your thoughts, neither are your ways my ways, declares the LORD. For as the heavens are higher than the earth, so are my ways."

Ask:

What does this verse say about God?

Ask:

What should we do if we disagree with God about something?

> If we trust that God is the Creator and He is good, then we need to realize that anytime we disagree with God, He is right and we are wrong. But, God welcomes and delights in us being honest and asking Him hard questions. We need to be honest with God about our thoughts and ask Him to transform our mind (Romans 12:1-2). Ask the Holy Spirit to help transform your mind. We cannot fix our mind on our own, but as we spend time in the Word of God, we can allow the Holy Spirit to transform our mind and heart.

Ask:
- Are we willing to ask God to transform us according to His truth? Are we willing to submit to Him as Lord? He is a Good Master that we can trust.

DISCUSSION QUESTIONS FROM THE *STUDY*

For the remainder of the time, discuss what the ladies got from the *Study* that week. Begin by opening the floor for them to be able to share things that stood out to them.

Possible discussion questions. The questions below all come straight from the *Study*, so hopefully the ladies in your group already have answers. Hopefully the discussion will become more than just people reading their written answers. Ask some of them to expound upon what they wrote or let others respond or ask questions. You probably will not have time to discuss all of the questions, so pray through which ones you want to start with. Be willing to

Detailed Leader's Guides for All Group Meetings: Week Two

be flexible if the Holy Spirit steers the group in a different direction than you planned. These questions are here to be a guide, but feel free to use your own questions as well.

Day 1

What are some areas of your life that you may still need to invite God into? Is there any reason you are reluctant to invite God into these areas?

> Remind the ladies that God cares about each of these areas. If they are sinful, he desires to cleanse and transform them. If there are areas of fear, 1 Peter 5:6-7 states, "Humble yourselves, therefore, under the mighty hand of God so that at the proper time he may exalt you, [7] casting all your anxieties on him, because he cares for you."

Day 2

Based on the gospel, how does God view you? How has your perspective of God's view of you changed this past week, if at all?

> Remember, God's view of them does not depend on their actions this past week. Because of the cross, God looks on them with love, favor, and a desire to be in relationship with them. Whether they had a great week or a rough week, God's view of them is based on Jesus' righteousness, not their behavior. I know we are being repetitive with this; however, this is such an important point to get across.

Day 3

Use your own words to explain why all sexual thoughts and activity that do not conform to God's intention grieve Him.

> God's design is good and sacred. When we go outside of God's design, we are allowing destructive sin into our lives. God is the biggest advocate for your current and/or future marriage. He desires what is best for you, and it grieves Him when you choose things that put a wedge between your relationship with Him and which jeopardizes your relationships with others.

Read Ephesians 5:25-33. What strikes you and why?

Day 4

Steps to Freedom: (1) Trust God's way is better; (2) Repent and cry out to God for rescue; (3) Turn your heart to God with love and affection; (4) Cling to God when your thoughts try to steer you back toward darkness.

    a. Which of these have you been able to live out this past week?

b. Which of these steps is hardest for you? Why?

Why is it important to realize that sex was never meant to be an individual endeavor? How does that differ from what society tells us today?

> God designed sex to be an expression of love between a husband and wife. It is an expression of intimacy and was never intended for individual pleasure or selfishness. Selfishness is in complete rivalry with love.

Day 5

Do we realize we are in a war? What are some tactics of Satan that stood out in this reading?

Read Romans 8 and name some of the promises.

Before Closing

If there is time, ask the ladies if there were any other insights from the *Study* that they wanted to discuss or questions they wanted to ask. If anyone asks a question to which you do not have an answer, it is sufficient to say, "I don't know, but will look into it for next time."

CLOSING PRAYER

Always reserve the last ten to fifteen minutes for prayer. Tell them,

- As we prepare to go to the Lord in prayer, answer this question in your heart, "Do I want to be humble and repentant?" Talk to God in prayer right now about this, making decisions and commitments, as well as a time of confession and repentance. Now tell the women that you will all go around the room in prayer and that you will start and then close the prayer time.

  > Be a role model in prayer. With heartfelt words, confess pride or selfishness in your life as well as any specific sins. Be open, honest, and vulnerable. Also share any commitments you are making. Give each woman an opportunity to confess her sins and pour out her heart to the Lord.

HOMEWORK

Tell the women to work through the *Study* and meet back again next week. They should also be sure to share exciting truths with their spouses and with others.

SELF-CRITIQUE OF MEETING

After the meeting is over, go over the standard critique outline listed in Week One. Focus especially upon whether you encouraged the women to participate or dominated the time with teaching. Pay special attention to whether each woman participated. Plan to make improvements next week.

SEND A TEXT TO THE WOMEN

Be sure to send a text or an email to each of the women this week. Below is an example of something you could share.

I enjoyed meeting with you this week. I am excited to be part of your life and watching you grow. I am here for you. I am praying for you. Please call me anytime you need to talk or just want me to pray with you. Keep at it. I believe in you.

Passionate for God,
Repentant in spirit,
Open and honest,
Victorious in living,
Eternal in perspective, and
Networking with other *Proven Women.*

MEMORY VERSE

2 Timothy 2:22 "So flee youthful passions and pursue righteousness, faith, love, and peace, along with those who call on the Lord from a pure heart."

WEEK  (based on Week Two *Study* materials)

Continue the practice of hugging each woman as she enters, and have each woman hug others in the group too.

OPENING PRAYER

After spending some time greeting one another, open with prayer. Invite God to join the group and ask Him to guide the discussion.

SINGING

Each night, be prepared to sing one song. Encourage the women to look up the lyrics on their phones.

CHECK-IN (Confession, God Stories, Emotions)

Begin the discussion by doing your weekly check-in. This check-in should include any confessions from the week, any God stories from the week, and how they are doing emotionally, both now and during the week.

After a lady confesses a setback, it is important to have her evaluate how she felt during the time of the setback and immediately after the setback. For instance, she may have felt ashamed or discouraged or even angry at herself. She may have even felt angry at God because she blames Him for allowing her to fall. The important part is that they are honest with how they felt. But then it is good to remind them of God's grace and forgiveness. They may have moved from shame and regret to gratitude and peace within the same day as they transitioned their focus

Proven Women: The Leader's Guide

from their sin to God's grace. These emotional transitions are so good to process together as a group because it teaches the ladies how to process their emotions on their own during the week with the Lord. Ask the women to turn to the *Feelings Chart* in Appendix F of the *Study* if that will help them articulate their emotions.

> Go around and let each woman share. Feel free to ask questions if she is not expounding on her own.

GOD STORIES

If they are having a hard time coming up with God stories on their own, you may ask them something like:

- How did you see God come through for you this week?
- Was there a time He gave you the strength to resist a temptation?
- Did you experience His love this week?
- Did he reveal something new about Himself through His Word?

Let's celebrate ways God is active in your life!

THOUGHT LIFE

Ask:

How did you guys do with your thought life this past week? Are you able to recognize lust at the thought level? Are you turning to repentance even when the lust is just thoughts and not actions?

> After allowing the women to share, mention that the goal of a Proven Woman is not merely to stop looking at pornography or masturbating, but to strive for absolute purity and a clean heart and mind. Sin begins in the mind, and when we allow impure thoughts to remain in our heads, it is just a matter of time before we act them out.

DISCUSSION/TEACHING

MEMORY VERSE

Ask someone to recite or read the weekly memory verse, 2 Timothy 2:22.

Detailed Leader's Guides for All Group Meetings: Week Three

Ask:

Why do you think it is important to both flee youthful passions and pursue Christ?

Give time for the ladies to share.

State:

Keep this verse in mind as we discuss this question: What are the greatest two commandments in Scripture?

Allow time for responses.

Read Matthew 22:36-40.

Matthew 22:36-40 "Teacher, which is the greatest commandment in the Law?"

[37] Jesus replied: "'Love the Lord your God with all your heart and with all your soul and with all your mind.'[a] [38] This is the first and greatest commandment. [39] And the second is like it: 'Love your neighbor as yourself.'[b] [40] All the Law and the Prophets hang on these two commandments."

State:

So, we can see from these verses that God's greatest desire for us is that we love God and love others. Everything should be done in love. Loving God also includes worshiping Him and honoring Him as Lord. Loving others includes putting their interests before our own and living in selflessness. First John 4:19 says, "We love because He first loved us." God does not just expect us to be able to love on our own. We love because we are first so loved by Him. He invites us into an intimate love relationship with Him that then overflows into our relationships with others. The whole reason we exist is for an intimate relationship with God. That is pretty incredible; the Lord wants a close friendship with you! He has called you both His daughter and His friend.

State:

Feel free to state this in your own words.

God is not satisfied sitting in heaven watching your life from a distance. He does not say, "Oh, good. Sara doesn't masturbate anymore," or "Ah, yes. She did not look with lust or fantasy during that movie sex scene." God wants to have a relationship with you. He wants you to talk to Him about everything. He wants you to tell Him of your struggles with lust, to tell Him of your worries, to ask Him for help, to talk about your desires and

Proven Women: The Leader's Guide

needs, and to tell Him you love Him. Do you see this? Does this help you understand how God wants you to act toward Him?

> Allow a response.

State:

> Feel free to state this in your own words.

These descriptions of God's desire for intimacy with his creation help show why it's not enough that we have a goal to stop masturbating or committing other sexual sins. God created us to have a relationship with Him, not just to do good works. It's not enough just to stop sexual sins. God wants us to have an intimate daily relationship with Him. Until we do, we will always have something missing in our lives that we will try to fill with something, such as sex, fantasies, hobbies, etc.

State:

Let's look again at 2 Timothy 2:22: "So flee youthful passions and pursue righteousness, faith, love, and peace, along with those who call on the Lord from a pure heart." We are called to both flee and pursue. We are to pursue God because that is our purpose and greatest commandment. However, we cannot do this freely if we are not also fleeing youthful passions.

During this week's study, we learned that we have two root problems from which all sin stems. What are those two roots? (selfishness and pride)

Ask:

How can selfishness and pride get in the way of pursuing God?

> Let them discuss. Also, a possible answer is that pride keeps us from loving and submitting to God because we want to do everything in our own strength rather than turning to God. Selfishness keeps us from putting others before ourselves and loving others. These two roots directly fight against God's commandment to love Him and others.

Tell the women:

Now, let me tell you a bit about why people commit sexual sins. Look at your hand right now. Do you see the five fingers? They all are connected to the palm of your hand. Imagine that your index finger is lust, the next finger is masturbation, the next is greed, the next pornography, and the final one is jealousy.

> Demonstrate using your hand and fingers.

Some people can bend over a finger and stop masturbating for a long time out of sheer determination. Maybe some can even bend over two fingers.

Ask:

But what do you see remaining?

> Let them answer.

State:

Yes, there are still other fingers of sin in your life. Chances are pretty good that something like fear will pop up where the bent finger was. We still have a problem because the root source of these sins is still there.

> Point to the palm.

State:

There is a root cause of lust, pornography, masturbation, and even jealousy and anger. All of these things stem from selfishness and the pride that goes along with it. That's right—the root sin is selfishness. As long as you have selfishness and pride, you will always be a slave to some form of sexual sin or other things like jealousy and anger, because these are all fed by selfishness. As you examine yourself and allow God to open your eyes, it will become more and more obvious just how much selfishness and pride exist in your life.

> Pause.

State:

The real question is: How do you stop being selfish and prideful? You cannot just do this on your own. It takes the power of Christ. Consider His hands.

Ask:

When He was nailed to the cross, what happened to His hands?

> Allow an answer.

Proven Women: The Leader's Guide

State:

Yes, there was a nail pierced right through His hand. This is an excellent example of how we can be set free from selfishness and pride. If we die to self and replace our hands with God's, we have a big hole right where selfishness and pride used to be.

Indicate by drawing a circle in the middle of your palm.

State:

The root source has been killed. Each moment you allow Jesus to live through you, you won't lust. You'll have new desires and experience freedom and joy.

State:

God gave of Himself so that you could live forever in heaven with Him. However, He wants you to live free from bondage now. You have heard the saying that we must die to self and that we must pick up our cross each day. How do you do this?

Allow a response.

State:

Here are some ways to help explain what these teachings mean: To let Jesus live for you… to yield your life completely to God… to stop living for selfish pleasures… to become one with God and take on His hands.

State:

The only way you can hope to stop living for yourself, yield to God, and rely completely upon Him is to decide, from this day on, that you will partner with Christ. We must daily invite Christ into our lives and resolve to be quick to repent whenever we see ourselves turning away. This is a real and persistent commitment. You need to have an attitude that makes you willing to stretch as high as possible and willing to do whatever it takes to be with God and to experience His healing.

Ask:

How about it: Are you willing to do whatever it takes to live in freedom and to be holy because God is holy?

State:

You must focus on God and make Him the center of your life. Only then will you stop pursuing lust or masturbation. The hole in your hand will be there the same as it is for Christ. In fact, the by-product of this relationship with God is that you won't keep turning to sexual sins. Again, if your goal is to be with God, not merely to stop a certain sin, you will be set free from sin. Holiness is an end result of living for Him.

State:

Do you see the big picture now? Do you see that living out the purpose for which God created you and choosing to live for Him is the cure for overcoming the sinful roots of selfishness and pride?

> Pause and allow an answer.

DISCUSSION QUESTIONS FROM THE *STUDY*

You probably will not have time to discuss all of the questions, so pray through which ones you want to start with. Be willing to be flexible if the Holy Spirit steers the group in a different direction than you planned for. These questions are here to be a guide, but feel free to use your own questions as well.

State:

Our purpose in life is to pursue a loving, intimate relationship with Christ. That is also the purpose of this study. This week discussed the (a) root problem of sin; (b) abiding in Christ; (c) fleeing and pursuing; (d) being passionate for God; and (e) repentant in spirit.

Does anyone want to start out by sharing anything that stood out to them this week?

Day 1
1. Read Galatians 5:16-25 and compare the works of the flesh versus the fruit of the Spirit. Which of these would you want to see evident in your life?
2. Take some time to picture the relationships in your life. How are the works of the flesh and the fruit of the Spirit evident in your relationships? How are they affecting your relationships?

Day 2
3. Read John 15:1-11. Day Two we talked about Jesus being the vine and we are the branches. How does the picture of the branch connected to the tree compare to the picture of the hand?

Just like selfishness and pride fuel sin, abiding in Christ fuels fruit in our life. If we are not connected to Christ, we will not bear fruit. Apart from Him we can do nothing. Apart from Christ, we will only see works of the flesh.

Day 3

4. 2 Timothy 2:22 "flee and pursue." We are meant to both pursue Christ and flee temptation. How are you being strategic in being in the Word and pursuing Christ?

    Encourage the ladies to never skip the Bible reading during each day's study. If they do not have time to complete an entire day's homework, the best thing they can do is be in the Word because God's Word is so much more powerful than the words found within Proven Women.

5. Are there any boundaries that you need to set in order to starve the flesh?

    These boundaries could be apps, television shows, people they are hanging out with, music, etc.

Day 4

6. In Day Four, we began going through the PROVEN acrostic. Day Four was (P)assionate for God. We were asked to meditate on our favorite verse and write a psalm. Does anyone want to share their verse or a psalm that they wrote?

    Really encourage them to read their psalm out loud. Make sure you write a psalm and be willing to share yours. It is not about how eloquent they sound but how genuine it is toward the Lord.

Day 5

7. Read Revelation 2:1-5 – (R)epentant in Spirit

    REMEMBER > REPENT > RETURN—Take some time to think of a time when you were closer to God. What were some things that were different about your life then? What changed?

8. During the week, we were asked to repent of anything that we allowed to come between us and the Lord. Is there anything that anyone wants to share with the group? Anything you still need to repent of?

    Give the ladies time to think. Some may need to confess and repent for the first time. Some may have repented during the week and want to share with the group what they repented of.

Detailed Leader's Guides for All Group Meetings: Week Three

Read Revelation 2:18-29. What comes to mind when you read this passage?

> This passage is really hard to read because it shows God's heart toward sexual sin. But there is a beautiful truth in this passage as well. God is calling us toward repentance. God is asking us not to harden our heart and refuse to repent.

CLOSING PRAYER

Reserve the last ten to fifteen minutes for prayer.

HOMEWORK

Tell the women to start recognizing what they are dwelling upon during the week and to keep notes. Encourage them to set a guard at the door to take captive all thoughts. Finally, ask them to think through what is holding them back from yielding all areas of their lives to the Lord.

SELF-CRITIQUE OF MEETING

Review the detailed critique from Week One.

PREPARATION FOR NEXT WEEK

Before the next group, review your notes from the week and write out an outline for the evening.

Proven Women: The Leader's Guide

SEND A TEXT TO THE WOMEN

Most of us have asked God to take away the temptation to lust. Why doesn't God answer that prayer? First, we grow through trials. We need to develop perseverance in order to be complete and mature (James 1:2–3). Second, we wouldn't turn to God if we never struggled or had any problems too big for us. We would never see ourselves as needy, dependent servants if we didn't need him to overcome some big thing in our lives. Finally, see turning to Jesus to overcome temptations as a spiritual act of worship, not a punishment (Romans 12:1–2). Be glad that you know what your daily cross is, and gladly walk with Jesus who says He carries the load when we turn it over to Him (Matthew 11:30).

MEMORY VERSE

Psalm 101:1-2 "I will sing of steadfast love and justice; to you O Lord, I will make music. I will ponder the way that is blameless. Oh when will you come to me? I will walk with integrity of heart within my house."

WEEK 4 (based on Week Three *Study* materials)

Be sure to show real love and concern for the women as you lead. Before praying, tell each of the women how happy you are that each of them is there. Point out that there are many women who need to be in a group like this one but choose not to. For the women in your group, their choice to participate in the group is an answer to God's call. Being called by God is a big step already! Tell the women these things, and commit to being an encourager as you lead the group.

OPENING PRAYER

Mention each woman by name as you pray. Make sure to invite God into the group and dedicate the time to Him.

SINGING/WORSHIP

Have one song prepared. Before the night begins, spend some time in personal prayer asking God to put a particular song on your heart. Each week, try to find a song that goes along with the theme of that week. This week focused a lot on repentance and having our thoughts fixed on Christ.

CHECK-IN

Ask the women to turn to the *Feelings Chart* in Appendix F of the *Study* and describe their feelings now or how they felt during the week.

> Allow each woman several minutes to discuss her week.

Proven Women: The Leader's Guide

GOD STORIES and CONFESSION

Ask:

- Ladies, I'd like to open the floor for both God stories as well as confessions for this past week. How did this past week go? How can we celebrate God's activity in your life? What needs to be brought before the Lord in confession?

DISCUSSION/TEACHING

State:

- This week we are continuing the PROVEN acrostic. Let's start by reviewing the letters.

    State each letter and ask if anyone can remember what it stands for.

> **P**assionate for God,
>
> **R**epentant in spirit,
>
> **O**pen and honest,
>
> **V**ictorious in living,
>
> **E**ternal in perspective, and
>
> **N**etworking with others

State:

Let's remember what a PROVEN woman looks like. A PROVEN woman is **P**assionately following God. She recognizes that she has sin in her heart and **R**epents to God, bowing in humility before him. She is **O**pen and honest with herself, God, and trusted friends. In fact, as she learns to trust God even more she is willing to dig a little deeper into her heart not fearing what is below the surface. If it is sinful, God will cleanse it and forgive it. If it is painful, God will bring comforting love and care while healing it. She begins to see **V**ictory in her choices, celebrating those victories with God who she recognizes is right beside her and powering every step. As she grows closer with God, she is often reminded to have an **E**ternal perspective. She loves God so much that she cannot wait for the day she will know him fully when she sees him face-to-face. Yet while here on this earth, she knows she has purpose as she continues to grow to know God more and make him known to others. She **N**etworks with other women who continue to encourage her and hold her up while she is weak and she also gets to encourage other women who are on this journey with Christ. She is PROVEN yet she is human. She will mess up. She will be disappointed, and experience trials and hardships. At times life will be mundane and boring. There will be times she wants to throw in the towel. But Christ will be with her to encourage her, comfort her, strengthen her, refine her, and pick her back up. She never has to do this alone. And if she forgets that and tries to, He will remind her.

God desires this for each one of us!!

This past week, the *Study* discussed repentance, openness, victorious living, and eternal perspective. Before we dive in, was there anything from this week that stood out for any of you?

> Give a few minutes for the ladies to catch up and share some things that they learned.

MEMORY VERSE

Ask someone to recite this week's memory verse, Psalm 101:1-2.

> Allow them to read it if they have not memorized it. Keep reminding them that it is important to be memorizing the weekly verses.

Ask:

In this Psalm, David begins by declaring his worship to the Lord. Why is having a heart of worship a good goal to have? Why is this a better goal than just to overcome lust and pornography?

> This is part of our design. We were created to worship God. When our minds are full of evil thoughts, our minds are not free to worship God. We are not just reclaiming our minds from lust, but we are reclaiming our minds for worshiping God.

State:

This verse also states, "I will ponder the way that is blameless." There is a difference between a fleeting thought and dwelling thoughts. This verse uses the word "ponder." To ponder means to think about something carefully or deliberately. When lustful thoughts come to mind, are you deliberately turning them toward something blameless, or are you allowing your mind to dwell on sexual fantasies? Remember, we will not have the willpower on our own to take our thoughts captive. But, when you turn to God in that moment, He will empower you to turn away from the sinful thought and free your mind to turn to Him in worship.

Proven Women: The Leader's Guide

Ask:

Sometimes we are not even aware of how often our mind turns to dwell on sinful things until we choose to be intentional with our minds. How would you say your thought life was this past week? Did you take notice of how often lustful thoughts and urges bombarded your mind? If you didn't notice, how can you be intentional this coming week to be aware of how your mind is doing?

> Give the ladies some time to talk about how this past week's thought life was. Also, have them brainstorm together how they could be more intentional about it this week if they were not intentional this past week. I had a girl once start to keep a daily tally of how many times she had sexual thoughts pop into her mind. She had no idea how immersed her mind was in lustful thoughts until she began taking note. Becoming aware of her thoughts helped her to take those thoughts captive. She began bringing them before the Lord rather than being a slave to whatever popped into her mind. If we do not take control of our mind, our mind will control us. If we do not take our thoughts captive according to 2 Corinthians 10:5, we will instead be held captive by them.

Ask:

Sometimes it is not that we are unaware of our thoughts, but that we deliberately choose to go down the path toward sexual fantasy or other sexual sins. If you had moments this week of choosing to ponder on sexual things, what kept you from turning to God in those moments for freedom?

> Give the ladies a few minutes to share. If no one says anything, here are a few possible answers: (1) too ashamed to turn to God in the moment, frustrated that I am struggling again; (2) enjoying the thoughts and really don't want them to end; (3) allowing myself this one last time, I will take them captive next time; (4) feeling like I have gone too far into the fantasy, I might as well finish it.

State:

If you haven't already memorized this past week's verse, please continue to commit it to memory. If you have memorized it, continue meditating on it throughout this week. Hopefully, with this verse at the forefront of your mind, you will experience God's conviction as lustful thoughts surface, pointing you to Christ. We really need to wage war against our mind and reclaim it for worship.

One way that may be helpful when it comes to memorizing the memory verse and keeping God's word at the front of your mind is to make the memory verse for the week the lock screen on your phone. Try it this week and see if it helps you memorize the verse and avoid some tempting situations.

Hopefully we all had a great week, but I'm sure each of us have had areas where we fell short. This is a great segue into the discussion questions for the week since the first day was about confession and repentance.

Before we jump into the discussion questions, I want to make sure we understand the difference between shame and conviction. Both feelings can take place once we have sinned and both move us into action. Shame is this sinking feeling that we feel after we've sinned that causes us to feel like we need to hide from God. We see Adam and Eve react this way in Genesis after they had sinned. That was an appropriate response for them because they had not experienced redemption through Christ. Shame is appropriate for anyone who has not put their faith in Christ because they cannot stand before God as they are. Shame, however, is not a proper response for believers. Instead of shame, we should feel conviction. Conviction is an invitation from the Lord to turn to Him in repentance. Christ has paved the way for us to come before God as we are. He paves the way for us to enter into God's presence so that we can confess our sins and therefore be cleansed and forgiven of the sins. Christ, our great high priest, is our advocate and gives us a right to stand before God. So, when there is sin in your life, do not listen to the accuser who is tempting you to stay away from God out of shame. Rather listen to your Redeemer who is calling you to repentance and restoration.

DISCUSSION QUESTIONS FROM THE *STUDY*

For the remainder of the time, discuss homework from the week. You probably will not have time to discuss all of the questions, so pray through which ones you want to start with. You can also begin by asking the ladies if anything from the first day jumped out to them. Move from day to day, either allowing them to share what moved them or asking the questions below. Let this be a guide but allow the Holy Spirit to lead the discussion. Answers have been provided, but also feel free to share any truths God has also shown you.

Day 1

1. Read Psalm 32. What are your initial thoughts of this passage?

    "For when I kept silent, my bones wasted away through my groaning all day long for day and night your hand was heavy upon me; my strength was dried up as by the heat of summer." What is this verse describing? (answer: conviction)

2. Although conviction is miserable, why is it such a good gift from God?

It is a gift because it is meant to draw us away from sin and toward God. It is meant to lead us to repentance which restores our relationship with God. If God did not give us conviction, we would most likely remain in sin and away from God. Do not confuse conviction with shame. Shame makes people want to hide from God. Conviction is God's invitation to repentance. Unfortunately, people often hide rather than return to God in repentance.

3. Why do you think it is important to not only confess to God but to also confess to others?

It brings the sin to light in a way that will bring accountability. Also it helps us overcome our pride. It is so easy to keep sin hidden so that we can have an appearance of godliness. Confessing sin sheds light onto it and also brings someone else into the fight against sin with us.

4. Is there anything anyone wants to share about how repentance has impacted their life in the past couple weeks since we started this study?

Give them a minute to share.

Day 2

5. Read Hebrews 12:1-13. Let them share their initial thoughts.

Verse 3 says to "consider him who endured such opposition from sinners, so that you will not grow weary and lose heart." What did Christ endure?

He endured the physical pain of the cross, the ridicule of man, and the wrath of God.

How does Christ's suffering empower us?

He endured the cross so that He could conquer sin and death for us. Because of what He did on the cross, we have His Spirit and therefore His power within us to say no. He endured such hostility to give us the ability to resist. And when we resist with His strength, we will not grow weary. When we remember what He did on our behalf, it is a reminder of how much He deserves our worship and gratitude.

6. Verses 5-11 speak of discipline. What is the difference between discipline and punishment?

Punishment is about justice, giving the person what they deserve. Discipline is for the good of the person, training them in the way they should go. God disciplines us out of love, not vengeance. He placed his wrath and the punishment on Jesus on the cross.

Day 3

7. Read 2 Corinthians 10:3-5 and Hebrews 4:14-16. Let them share their initial thoughts.

Satan wants you to believe that you are unable to go to God when you are dealing with temptations. He is the accuser, making you feel ashamed. Have there been any particular thoughts that come to mind when you are being tempted that make you think you can't turn to God?

> Possible answers: You are too dirty to go to God, He is mad at you and will ignore you. You are a disappointment to God. You are not worth His time. You've done it too many times for Him to forgive you this time, etc.

How do you know these are lies?

> God says we can come to Him in our time of need and break off any shame we may feel.

Day 4

8. Read Psalm 101.

    This day was much more contemplative. It may be best to have everyone turn to these pages in the book and walk through this day together and share answers. Let the ladies share whatever answers they desire to share.

9. After reading Psalm 101, are there any forms of media/entertainment that God is asking you to give up?

Day 5

10. Eternal Perspective – Read Psalm 16. Let them share initial thoughts.
    a. Are there any circumstances that are stealing your joy right now?
    b. Take some time to discuss what it will be like once we are all in heaven, no more tears or regrets.
    c. Now come back to your present circumstances and view them through the lens of eternity and the inheritance that Jesus promises. Is there anything about your perspective that has changed? Is there anything for which you can be grateful?

CLOSING PRAYER

Always reserve the last ten to fifteen minutes for prayer. Encourage all of the ladies to take turns praying. Also, ask the ladies to not only pray for one another but also to be willing to pray for themselves during group prayer. There is something so powerful about handing our own burdens to the Lord in the presence of others. It is very powerful to entrust ourselves to God and release that burden by faith.

HOMEWORK

Encourage the women to be watchful for opportunities to share with others what they are learning. They are a vessel that God can use to help others!

SELF-CRITIQUE OF MEETING

Review the critique outline from Week One. Did you encourage the women to participate, or did you dominate the time with teaching? Did each woman have enough time for sharing? Be sure to continually learn from your experiences each week. You will grow as a leader each week.

PREPARATION FOR NEXT WEEK

Be sure to read through the homework ahead of time so that you are mentally and spiritually prepared for next week. As you go through the homework, ask God to put a song on your heart for next week. Also, ask God to remind you of how He used this week's material to speak to your heart the first time you went through the *Study*. Be willing to share personally how God used His truth to transform you.

SEND A TEXT TO THE WOMEN

The biggest battle you will face in overcoming sexual sin is turning the focus off yourself and putting it onto God. God desires for us to fix our eyes onto Him in worship. Ask God to continually open your eyes to see Him more clearly and to fall in love with Him more and more. As our eyes fixate on Him, they will naturally turn from being fixated on ourselves. Love you ladies! Keep at it!

MEMORY VERSE

James 1:14 "But each person is tempted when he is lured and enticed by his own desire."

WEEK  (based on Week Four *Study* materials)

Remember to keep greeting the women with a hug.

OPENING PRAYER

After spending some time greeting one another, open with prayer. Remember, prayer is not just a way to open a group, but it is a time of dedicating this group session to the Lord. It is a time of inviting Him into the group and letting His Spirit lead the discussion.

SINGING

Each night, be prepared to sing one song. This can simply be done on your phone. You can either print out words or ask the ladies to look up the lyrics on their phone as well.

CHECK-IN

Ask the women to turn to the *Feelings Chart* in Appendix F of the *Study* and describe their feelings now or how they felt during the week. Have them describe how their battle for purity went throughout the week and how they felt in the midst of it. How did they feel during a hard time? How did they feel after? Remember, this helps them process their emotions so that they are able to bring these thoughts and feelings before the Lord throughout the week.

Proven Women: The Leader's Guide

GOD STORIES and CONFESSION

Ask:
- Ladies, I'd like to open the floor for both God stories as well as confessions for this past week. How did this past week go? How can we celebrate God's activity in your life? What needs to be brought before the Lord in confession?

> We are now a third of the way through the *Study*. Hopefully, you are seeing your ladies begin to open up more. Our prayer is that when there are setbacks, there is true repentance and a desire to "go and sin no more." Do you have any ladies who repent of the same setbacks each week and do not seem to care? Or who seem really frustrated that they cannot get victory? If either of these are the cases, be willing to spend time in prayer as a group. If one doesn't seems to be broken over her sin, spend time praying for conviction; that He will help her see the sin the way He sees it and truly desire victory. If one seems frustrated, pray that God will give her the strength to withstand in the midst of the temptation in the coming week. Pray that God will show her how He is providing a way out each time (1 Corinthians 10:13). Let these ladies know that you desire to help them walk toward freedom and are willing to be available for accountability during the week.

DISCUSSION/TEACHING

MEMORY VERSE

Ask someone to recite this week's memory verse, James 1:14.

> Ask them to share how this verse impacted their lives this week. Give them a few minutes to share. Be ready to share your own experiences to get the conversation going if no one speaks up at first.

State:

Let's look at another verse. Psalm 37:4, "Delight yourself in the Lord and He will give you the desires of your heart." Notice that both James 1:14 and Psalm 37:4 mention desires.

State:
- This week we really started to dig into the heart of lust and into our own hearts as well. The first couple weeks we really hit on how we were created to love and worship God. Our hearts were designed to propel us toward God. Unfortunately, they get distracted so easily. There are so many longings within our hearts, some good and some evil. We

can see the contrast in these two verses we just mentioned. James 1 states that it is our desires that tempt us, revealing how our desires can be evil. Psalm 37 tells us that when we delight in the Lord, he gives us the desires of our heart, which means they would be good desires that line up with His.

The thing most vital is that we need to be intentional about steering our heart rather than allowing our heart to steer us. If left unattended, our heart will be overcome with selfish and prideful desires. Our heart will lead us toward a bottomless pit that cannot be fulfilled. As we give our heart over to the Lord, he refines and transforms it into a heart that loves and seeks Him.

State:

Women desire to be found beautiful, to be chosen, to be adored, to be needed, protected, valued and found irreplaceable. Those are all good desires to have, and many women would agree that they resonate with them. The thing is, our hearts often get confused and chase after the wrong things to fill those desires.

> The good news is, there are verses in the Bible that show us how Christ is the only one who can fulfill each of our desires, and His grace gives us the opportunity to run back to Him and allow Him to fulfill us in a way that nothing else can.

State:

In the beginning, God designed our hearts to long for Him. Our hearts were meant to propel us toward Him and toward one another in a pure and loving manner. Even though we do not get to live in God's original design, devoid of sin and heartache, He still has a beautiful design for us today. God designed the family to be a safe and nurturing place. Little girls are meant to be loved and protected by their fathers and nurtured by their mothers. As the little girl grows older, her parents teach her about God, Jesus, and the Holy Spirit. This young woman grows in confidence and security within her family; however, she finds her true identity in Christ. As she joins her life with Christ, He brings redemption to her broken soul and breathes true life into her. Her family and friends may disappoint her at times and this brings pain; however, her true worth and contentment are found in being the Adopted Daughter of the King of Kings. As she grows into a godly woman, she may be blessed with a husband and a family of her own. Her identity is not to be found in these things either, but they are an avenue to express her worship to the Lord as well as relationships she gets to enjoy and delight in. God delights in watching His daughters find joy!! She joins in covenant with a man, which symbolizes her covenant with Christ. They are to love and respect one another, enjoy one another, and come together in intimacy. Once again, her husband will at times disappoint her and sin against her and that will be painful, yet this will not shake her identity because her identity is still found in

Christ. She also will disappoint Him and sin against him, but God will bring mercy and reconciliation in those moments as well.

> This is God's design for today and it is beautiful. And the most beautiful thing is there is hope for everyone. Some little girls did not have a good experience with their fathers, while others do not even have a father at all. Some fathers do better than others; however, no father is perfect. No matter how wonderfully or how horribly our fathers loved us, we have hope because our true completion comes through Christ.
>
> The same is true about marriage. Some have an amazing marriage, some have a very difficult marriage, and some may never marry. We all have hope because we are not completed by our husbands, but through Christ.

Ask:

After hearing this design by God, what brings you hope?

Where do you see this design playing out in your life?

Why is it important to find our identity in God rather than in another person?

> When we find our identity in someone else, we lose our foundation and identity if they hurt us or leave us. Our identity and life will be dependent on someone that is not reliable. When we put our foundation and identity in who we are in Christ, it remains stable because God will never leave us nor forsake us.

Why is it hard to not try to find our identity in someone else?

> If we do not truly believe that God loves us and accepts us, we will try to find our acceptance/worth somewhere else. Also, if we do not love God with all of our heart, then we will not cherish the fact that He loves and accepts us. When we desire someone's approval more than we desire God's approval, we have allowed that person to become an idol in our life, and we are giving them control over our life. God wants to be our first love!

DISCUSSION QUESTIONS FROM THE *STUDY*

You probably will not have time to discuss all of the questions, so pray through which ones you want to start with. Be willing to be flexible if the Holy Spirit steers the group in a different direction than you planned for. These questions are here to be a guide, but feel free to use your own questions as well.

Detailed Leader's Guides for All Group Meetings: Week Five

Day 1

1. Read through the following passages (or pick a few to read): Galatians 5:18-24, Jeremiah 17:9, 2 Peter 1:4, Ephesians 2:1-3, Romans 7:5, Romans 8:5-10, 1 Peter 4:1-6, 1 John 2:15-17.

    After reading these passages, what are your thoughts on desire's role in temptation?

    How do these passages contradict what society is teaching us about following your heart no matter where it leads?

    > Today's culture is very determined to convince people to follow their own heart. The Bible warns us that our desires are wicked and selfish. They will steer us toward destruction. It is vital that we listen to God's truth rather than society. God's truth needs to be the loudest voice in our lives. His Word needs to be what we submit our lives to rather than submitting our lives to our own opinions or the opinions of society.
    >
    > Remember, during Week Two we discussed the importance of God's Word being more trustworthy than any other opinion, including our own. We have to ask ourselves if we are willing to align with God's truth, even if it goes against what our heart longs for.

2. Are there any desires that you are allowing to reign over you?

Day 2

3. What is the difference between a longing and a pursuit?

    > A longing is a desire of our heart, such as to be loved, accepted, belong, etc. A pursuit is the avenue in life we use to attempt to fulfill that longing, such as marriage, career, fame, etc.

4. Why do you think God doesn't always fulfill our longing with the specific pursuit we are seeking?

    > We are designed to long for God and love Him with all of our heart. If God chose to fulfill each of these desires in a tangible way on this earth every time we desired or asked Him for something, then we would see Him as a great genie who always gives us what we want rather than seeing Him as a holy, righteous God who deserves our allegiance, love, and affection.

5. What are you doing to stir your affection for the Lord?

Day 3

6. John 15:5 says, "apart from me you can do nothing." Do you fully believe that you cannot do any of this apart from God?

7. Why is it tempting to fix ourselves on our own?

   There could be differing answers, but it is in our nature to want to fix ourselves. It can be a form of control. It can also be us rivaling with God, wanting to do it ourselves rather than have to submit ourselves to God. It could possibly show a lack of faith, not expecting God to come through on our behalf. They also could have a completely different answer.

8. What is holding you back from relying completely on God and relinquishing your self-effort?

Day 4

9. Read Isaiah 14:12-20 and Ezekiel 28:11-19 and discuss how selfishness and pride contributed to the fall of Satan. What stands out to you about Satan before his fall and after?

   He was perfect in beauty yet still wanted more. In attempting to ascend higher and higher on his own, he ended up falling completely and losing all that he had.

10. Do you ever feel "not beautiful enough"? What does it take for you to consider yourself "beautiful enough"?

11. How does selfishness and pride distort our desire to be "beautiful enough"?

    For many, beautiful enough is to be "fairest of them all." It is a desire to outdo or outshine everyone else. There is a desire to build oneself up and tear everyone else down. This is a very divisive desire.

12. After reading the passages about Satan's fall, is there anything that God has brought to light about your desire for beauty?

Day 5

13. Read Philippians 2:1-11 and discuss. How does Jesus' attitude contrast from Satan's?

14. How does this passage about Jesus contrast with Ezekiel's passage about Satan?

    Satan was perfect in beauty yet wanted more. He wasn't God yet wanted to be higher than God. Jesus is equal to God yet did not seek this. Rather, he emptied Himself and humbled Himself.

Detailed Leader's Guides for All Group Meetings: Week Five

What was God's response to Jesus' humility and obedience?

> God exalted Him.

What was God's response to Satan's selfishness and pride?

> God cast him away.

State:

Satan and society have distorted beauty. They say beauty = value = sexiness. Many girls feel they need to find their sex appeal to find their value. Has this concept impacted your view of yourself? Do you ever feel the need to find your sex appeal in order to increase your value as a person?

Ask:

What does God call praiseworthy? (Proverbs 31:30)

> A woman who fears the Lord

Ask:

What does God call imperishable beauty?

> 1 Peter 3:3-4 – a gentle and quiet spirit.

State:

Are you guys seeing why it is so important to know Scripture? Society really wants to define us; however, God is the only one who has the right to define us.

CLOSING PRAYER

Reserve about fifteen minutes for prayer. **Introduce a "popcorn style" of praying.** Tell the women that there are fifteen minutes for prayer and that each person should pray many times. Therefore, as each person prays, she should keep it short and to one topic. Tell them that each woman should jump in as she feels led and that everyone should pray several times. Tell them to be sure to pour out their hearts in prayer, confession, and adoration, letting the Lord lead them. Also, it is okay for there to be times of silence. Set the example with short, heartfelt prayers in between your ladies at times.

Proven Women: The Leader's Guide

HOMEWORK

Tell the women to write out a game plan for how they will address common situations where they are tempted or have had a setback in the past few months. Have them bring it to the next meeting. Remind them to keep doing the *Study* daily.

SELF-CRITIQUE OF MEETING

Did you encourage the women to participate, or did you dominate the time with teaching? Did each woman have enough time for sharing? Keep evaluating the meetings.

SEND A TEXT TO THE WOMEN

Call or text the women during the week to check in. Remind them to prepare a game plan and encourage them to write a psalm as well.

MEMORY VERSE

Hebrews 4:15-16 "For we do not have a high priest who is unable to sympathize with our weaknesses, but one who in every respect has been tempted as we are, yet without sin. Let us then with confidence draw near to the throne of grace, that we may receive mercy and find grace to help in time of need."

WEEK  (based on Week Five *Study* materials)

Hug each woman at the beginning and end of the meeting, and encourage the others to do the same.

OPENING PRAYER

After spending some time greeting one another, open with prayer. Feel free to ask if any of the ladies wants to be the one to open your time together in prayer.

SINGING

Each night, be prepared to sing one song together as a group. Try to find a song that goes with a truth that you learned from this past week.

CHECK-IN

Ask the women to turn to the *Feelings Chart* in Appendix F of the *Study* and ask how they are feeling now as well as how they felt throughout the week. What happened to cause them to feel that way? Are they learning to take their emotions to the Lord, knowing God cares for them? Praise God He has empathy and compassion toward us. When God calls us to rejoice with those who rejoice and mourn with those who mourn (Romans 12:15), be assured that this reflects God's heart toward us. He also mourns and rejoices alongside us because He cares.

Proven Women: The Leader's Guide

GOD STORIES and CONFESSION

Ask:

Ladies, I'd like to open the floor for both God stories as well as confessions for this past week. How did this past week go? How can we celebrate God's activity in your life? What needs to be brought before the Lord in confession?

> Give them each time to share. Remember, when people confess, remind them that God forgives and cleanses. Rather than ever telling someone that it is okay after they confess sin, tell them they are forgiven. It is not okay that we sin, but praise God that He always forgives and cleanses us of our sin because of what Jesus did on the cross. Always keep Christ the center of forgiveness.
>
> Be sure to celebrate God stories. Even if a woman has a setback, but she was able to resist several times because God gave her the strength in those other moments, celebrate those moments. Celebrate opportunities to share with others what God is teaching you.

DISCUSSION/TEACHING

MEMORY VERSE

Ask someone to recite this week's memory verse, Hebrews 4:15-16.

Ask:
- When can we run to God?

  > Give them a moment to answer.

State:
- The verse says we can run to God when we need mercy, which means we have the freedom to do so even in our sin. But let's make sure we are running to Him to receive mercy for our sin, not to receive affirmation for our sin. God is not going to say it is okay for you to remain in your sin. That is why we have time every week for confession and to talk about how to recognize patterns. So that we can be ridding ourselves of this sin. But we need God in order to be able to rid ourselves of sin. Praise God, He welcomes us in our time of need.

State:
- This week we are also going to dive in a bit deeper in our discussion about longings. Have any of you ever longed for something so much that you could feel the longing physically? We could be longing for something good or longing for something evil. Either way, longings can be deep and strong.

- Read Psalm 63.

State:
- Do you hear the longing in this passage? This is describing a time in David's life when he knew he was longing for God and how fulfilling it was to experience God in the midst of this longing. Trust me, David understands longing. He understands good longing and evil longing. During Week Three we read the account of how he longed for Bathsheba, resulting in adultery and murder. This same David now says his heart longs for God as in a dry land where there is no water. He now realizes what His heart truly is driven toward—GOD! And when He steers His heart toward God, that deep soul longing is fulfilled.

Jesus and the Woman at the Well

You should have read John 4 this week which is the story of Jesus' encounter with the woman at the well. Jesus points out her sin to her. He was not trying to be harsh or judgmental. In fact, this was the most loving thing Jesus could do for her. This woman was miserable. She came to the well every day at the hottest point of the day to avoid the other women of the village. She was lonely and ashamed. Jesus pointed it out for her because He wanted to restore her, not condemn her. He understood her heart even more than she did. He knew what would rejuvenate her—HIM! Remember, when God convicts us of sin, it is never to condemn us. When we confess our sin before God and to each other, it is not to air our dirty laundry or make us feel bad, but to reveal an area of our heart that needs God's loving touch. He desires to heal and restore.

DISCUSSION QUESTIONS FROM THE *STUDY*

You probably will not have time to discuss all of the questions, so pray through which ones you want to start with. Be willing to be flexible if the Holy Spirit steers the group in a different direction than you planned for. These questions are here to be a guide, but feel free to use your own questions as well.

Proven Women: The Leader's Guide

Day 1:

1. We just heard about Jesus' conversation with the woman at the well. Do you believe God understands the longings of your heart more than you do? If not, why is this hard to believe?

2. When Jesus met the woman, he pointed out that she had had multiple marriages and was now living with someone who was not her husband. If Jesus met you in person today, what are some things He might point out in your life?

    This question is very vulnerable. Be willing to share first if no one answers. Don't ask this question if you are not willing to answer it.

3. This woman at the well ran and shared her experience with Jesus with her town. Is there anyone with whom you need to share about how God is transforming your life so that they have hope that God can transform them too?

Day 2: Desire to be chosen

4. Rejection can be a very painful experience, and sometimes a defining experience. Is there any label that you carry that God never intended for you to carry?

    Single, not enough, disappointment, divorced, unseen, etc.

5. How is the desire to be chosen affecting your life? Good or bad?

    It could be pushing them toward God. It could be pushing them toward a good, healthy relationship. It could push them toward feeling desperate and depressed. It could cause them to settle for an unhealthy relationship or still be fueling sexual sin.

6. Read Isaiah 54:1-6 and discuss.

God says, "Fear not, for you will not be ashamed; be not confounded, for you will not be disgraced; for you will forget the shame of your youth, and the reproach of your widowhood you will remember no more. For your Maker is your husband, the Lord of hosts is his name; and the Holy One of Israel is your Redeemer, the God of the whole earth he is called. For the Lord has called you like a wife deserted and grieved in spirit, like a wife of youth when she is cast off."

This is the beautiful promise that God erases any disgraceful stigmas that we have. We may feel rejected and overlooked on this earth, and that is so painful. But God has taken away that shame and comforted your pain. This passage also says that he deserted us, but with great compassion he gathers us in. This is talking to the Israelites. When they, as an entire people, would reject God and turn to other gods, he would allow them to experience judgment from other countries. He would desert them. But He always returned in compassion, even if they didn't deserve it. For us, while we were still enemies of God, he saved us. Because of the cross, he will never desert us. He draws us in and removes our shame.

7. How does it feel to know that no matter how you have been treated by others, God claims you as His and removes shame and reproach?

Day 3:

8. We often use walls to guard our hearts from pain. Does anyone want to share what kinds of walls they use to guard their hearts?

    Some shut down all desires, some become numb through pornography, some stay busy, some jump from man to man so they never have to experience the pain.

9. Proverbs 4:23 "Guard your heart above all else for it is the wellspring of life." What is this verse asking us to gaurd our hearts from? (SIN!!)

10. What do we usually try to guard our hearts from?

    Pain, discomfort, rejection, hard times, insecurities, the unknown, etc.

11. How have you used pornography as a wall to protect your heart from pain, whether in the past or currently?

    Escape from current pain. Prevention from experiencing new pain. Remember, this can be either video, reading, other sexual sins like fantasizing or apps.

    Remind the ladies that God is the God of all comfort and He is the one who can protect and help them guard their hearts.

From Week 5 Day 4: God of all Comfort –

12. Read 2 Corinthians 1:3-11 and discuss what this passage says about God.

    God comforts us with His presence, with His strength, with empathy, by acknowledging our pain, by listening and caring. Which of these means the most to you?

13. Does anyone want to share about how God has been your comforter?

From Week 5 Day 5:

14. John 11 is the story of Jesus raising Lazarus from the dead. In verse 35, Jesus wept. He wept because he loved Mary and Martha and He knew how painful this experience

was for them. Before he fixed their situation, he grieved with them. Do you trust God enough to open your heart to Him? That He will grieve with you? Are there any layers of your heart that you consider still unavailable to God and/or others?

15. What holds you back from opening up about these areas?

> If anyone shares, thank them for trusting the group enough to share. Ask if you can pray over them. Also ask if they are willing to pray and give this over to God.
>
> Even if they do not want to open up today, spend some time praying for God to soften these areas of our hearts and teach us to trust Him more and more.

CLOSING PRAYER

Spend the last fifteen minutes in prayer. **Tonight, ask the women to kneel during prayer time and to meet with God for the purpose of drawing close to Him and of knowing Him.** Model a heartfelt prayer as you have each woman share from his heart in prayer.

HOMEWORK

Remind the women that sharing exciting truths with others is an important part of the healing process. For married women, regularly sharing with their spouse what they are learning in the *Study* and in the group will greatly encourage and strengthen them and help rebuild trust. Ask the women if they are becoming more open and vulnerable in discussions with others. Remind them that creating special times to meet with the Lord, such as prayer walks, meditating on the attributes of God, and writing notes to God, is equally important.

SELF-CRITIQUE OF MEETING

Spend a few minutes thinking how the meeting went. Are you getting to know the women? Are they feeling safe? Are they being open and honest?

Make sure you are ending the meetings on time. It is a great sign of respect and shows the women in your group how much you value them. It may also keep them from arriving home late, which can cause friction. Start on time and be willing to cut out some discussion. Remember, the suggested outlines in this guide likely will take longer than two hours if they are done in their entirety, so you must make choices. It will be your responsibility to ensure it remains a time of humility and true worship of the Lord.

PREPARATION FOR NEXT WEEK

Be sure to come to each meeting prepared by going through the week's guide prior to your meeting.

SEND A TEXT TO THE WOMEN

Send a personal text to each woman this week. Pray that God will give you the right words to encourage them.

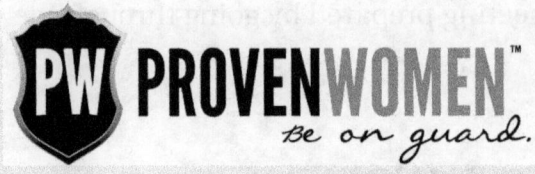

Passionate for God,
Repentant in spirit,
Open and honest,
Victorious in living,
Eternal in perspective, and
Networking with other *Proven Women.*

MEMORY VERSE

Philippians 2:3-5 "Do nothing from selfish ambition or conceit, but in humility count others more significant than yourselves. Let each of you look not only to his own interests, but also to the interests of others. Have this mind among yourselves, which is yours in Christ Jesus."

WEEK  7 (based on Week Six *Study* materials)

OPENING PRAYER

After spending some time greeting one another, open with prayer, dedicating this group session to the Lord. Invite God into the group and ask His Spirit to lead the discussion.

SINGING

Come prepared for a song to sing together as a group.

CHECK-IN

Ask the women to turn to the *Feelings Chart* in Appendix F of the *Study* and to describe their feelings now and how they felt during the week. Hopefully by now this has become a very natural routine, but be sure to ask them questions to help them expound and process their feelings. What caused you to feel that way? Were you able to express those feelings to God during the week? How did it affect your emotions to bring them before the Lord? Remember, we need to be honest about all of our emotions, good and bad. If we are having harmful feelings such as jealousy or greed, we should confess them before the Lord rather than attempt to bury them. When we confess our sin, he is faithful and just to forgive and cleanse our sins. Confession is our way of working through these emotions in order to bring them to a healthy place. With the help of the Holy Spirit, jealousy can transition into contentment and gratitude. Greed can transition into humility. But we need God's help with this.

Proven Women: The Leader's Guide

CONFESSION and GOD STORIES

Ask the women if they had any setbacks this week. Follow up with questions such as, "What led up to it, and how did you respond?" Keep the point before the women that confession needs to take place immediately for every sin. Ask the women to describe any faltering in their thought lives, such as lust, greed, fantasy, dreams, or jealousy. If they shared about these types of thoughts during the check-in, you do not need to rehash it all. However, if they did not open up about their emotions during their setbacks, this is a good time to talk about that as well.

Be sure to continually encourage the women to share victories each week. Remind them that these are called God stories because all victories come from God being at work in our lives. We cannot do this on our own for God. We have victory when we walk with God. Sharing God stories is a way of worship.

NOTE

This week may be more sensitive because of the topic of abuse. Statistically, it is very possible that someone in your group has experienced some form of abuse in the past. Remember, you are not a counselor. We do not expect you to act as a counselor. If it seems they need a counselor, encourage them to speak with one of the pastors at your church. You simply need to be willing to listen and be sensitive to what they are going through.

DISCUSSION/TEACHING

MEMORY VERSE

Ask someone to recite this week's memory verse, Philippians 2:3-5.

Ask:
- How have these verses impacted your lives this week?

    Be ready to share your own experiences to get the conversation going if no one speaks up at first.

State:
- This week we are going to continue with the desires of the heart, which include being protected and valued. But first, we are going to talk about having our minds transformed to Christ. We have been talking a lot about the heart lately. We are working to align our heart back to loving Christ. We also need to have the mind of Christ. Which brings us again to our memory verse: Philippians 2:3-5 " Do nothing from selfish ambition or

conceit, but in humility count others more significant than yourselves. ⁴ Let each of you look not only to his own interests, but also to the interests of others. ⁵ Have this mind among yourselves, which is yours in Christ Jesus."

- Throughout this study, we have seen that selfishness and pride are the root of lust and all other sin. In order to have the mind of Christ, we need to ask God to help us walk in humility in order to put others' needs before our own. These verses go on to say that Jesus is equal with God yet did not look for status, but rather became a servant. He humbled Himself to the point of death on the cross so that we could live. When we go to God in prayer, are we coming humbly and as a servant? Or are we being demanding, asking that our desires be met in our own way? What does it look like for our minds to be transformed into the mind of Christ?

- Read Romans 12:1-2. "I appeal to you therefore, brothers, by the mercies of God, to present your bodies as a living sacrifice, holy and acceptable to God, which is your spiritual worship. ² Do not be conformed to this world, but be transformed by the renewal of your mind, that by testing you may discern what is the will of God, what is good and acceptable and perfect."

- Let's break these verses down. Paul, as a spiritual leader, is pleading with them in these two verses. He is asking them to present themselves as a living sacrifice. Living sacrifice goes right along with Philippians 2:3-5. In order to be sacrificial, we cannot have selfish ambition or only look out for our own interests. A living sacrifice is living for something or someone beyond themselves. Paul wants us to present our bodies, holy and acceptable. This can only be done through Christ. Christ makes us holy and acceptable; yet, we have to willingly give ourselves to Him. This takes intentionality on our part of partnering with Christ.

- Second, Paul is pleading with us to not be conformed to the world but be transformed by the renewing of our mind. What does it look like to renew our mind? We need to be in God's Word daily, understanding that God's way probably is very different from the world that we see around us. Where our lives are not aligning with the Bible, we need to agree with the Bible and confess to the Lord how our lives fall short. Then we rely on the power of the Holy Spirit to help us choose God's ways over our own. This is why it is called living sacrifice. God's ways will often be different from what our hearts are desiring since they are naturally selfish. Yet, we can trust that if it is God's way, it is better for us. We just need to trust God more than we trust our own hearts.

- In Day One of this week's study, it spoke in detail about our brains and how they develop over time. It is as if our brains have roads in them that we develop with habitual actions.

Proven Women: The Leader's Guide

Our brains like to use the road most traveled. The only way to renew our mind is with deliberate, repetitive actions. That is why our heartwork is daily. If you have been doing your work daily for the past six weeks, then you are well on your way for rewiring your brain. If you have not been consistent, you are only halfway through the *Study*. You still have time to be making these things habits in your mind. This is part of the importance of getting daily into the Word. In the past or perhaps even still now, your mind wanted to constantly go to porn, fantasies, lustful reading. I am hoping now, as you have been daily getting into the Word, you are developing a new road in your brain that is frequently being used. This is part of transforming your mind.

- How has the homework been for you all? Are you able to be consistent in doing it each day? If you have been procrastinating and trying to do all of it the day before, let's be more intentional about making this a daily thing.

DISCUSSION QUESTIONS FROM THE *STUDY*

You probably will not have time to discuss all of the questions, so pray through which ones you want to start with. Be willing to be flexible if the Holy Spirit steers the group in a different direction than you planned for. These questions are here to be a guide, but feel free to use your own questions as well.

From Week 6 Day 1:

1. Read Philippians 2:1-11 and discuss.
2. What are some attributes of the mind of Christ?

    Humility, selflessness, sacrificial love.

3. Day One speaks of the brain and the roads most traveled (aka habits). What are the most well-worn paths in your brain? When you are going through a rough time, what is your go-to method of getting through it?

    Possible answers: Avoid it with busyness, TV, music, etc. Still turning to habits of masturbation and porn. Talking to a godly friend who will remind you of biblical truth and pray with you. Prayerfully bringing your situation to God and reading your Bible for answers. Food, alcohol, other indulgences.

    Any of these things can become a road in our brain. It will take intentionality over a period of time to change one of those roads from an unhealthy habit (masturbation, alcohol, etc.) to a healthy habit (prayer, meditation, Scripture). The important part is to realize that this transition is possible and to not give up.

4. How have you seen your thought processes change over the past six weeks?

From Week 6 Day 2: Desires for Protection

5. Sometimes we desire to be protected, not because we need the protection, but because we want to know that we are worth protecting. Are there any thoughts that pop into your mind that make you question your value?

    Be sensitive to the things that are shared. Even if what they feel is not true, it may seem very real to them. It is good to recognize thoughts that make us feel worthless so that we can replace them with God's truth. Jesus was willing to purchase each of us with His blood. He endured all of God's wrath so that we could be welcomed into a relationship with Him. If ever we question whether God loves us, we only need to look at the cross. If ever we question whether God is willing to protect us, we need only look at the cross. Even if we face difficult times while on this earth, God has protected us from spending all of eternity in hell. Romans 8:18, "For I consider that the sufferings of this present time are not worth comparing with the glory that is to be revealed to us."

6. What do you do when you have one of these thoughts?

    2 Corinthians 10:5 "We destroy arguments and every lofty opinion raised against the knowledge of God and take every thought captive to obey Christ."

    The more we know God's truth, the more we will able to recognize Satan's lies and be able to take those thoughts captive. God is a gentle, loving Father. His kindness is what will lead us to repentance. God is not a degrading accuser. He knows your value because He designed you. You are His creation and His image bearer. God loves you, and the more we remain in Him the more we will become who He designed us to be.

7. When we get thoughts of unworthiness, it is easy to allow our thoughts to spiral downward, feeling hopeless or depressed. It is easy to escape into lustful thoughts to make us feel better. Instead, we should think about how God sees us.

    Read Psalm 139 and discuss.

    No matter where you go, God is there. He sees every detail because He cares.

    You are fearfully and wonderfully made.

    If you run away, God will pursue.

    We are worth it in God's eyes. Even though He is the one who is worthy.

8. Think back through this past week. Did you have any downward thought spirals similar to what was presented in the *Study?* Are you more susceptible to lust in the midst of these thoughts?

Proven Women: The Leader's Guide

9. How can we be proactive in taking these thoughts captive?

    Don't just redirect your thoughts when they are full of lust. Redirect them toward Christ when they are untrue. You need to nip them in the bud even when they are not sexual, but threatening your worth in God's eyes. Remember, Satan is trying to destroy you.

From Week 6 Day 3: Protection continued.

10. Read Psalm 20 and discuss.

    Some trust in horses and chariots, but we trust in the name of the Lord our God. According to the *Study,* the desire for protection may stem out of desire to be valued. We want to know that someone loves us enough to protect us. God loves us more than we can imagine. Do we trust in His loving protection?

11. What might hold us back from trusting God for our protection?

    Perhaps he has allowed you to walk through really hard times. Maybe it's easier to trust in something that you see rather than to trust God.

    I can't guarantee that He will not keep you from walking through a really hard circumstance. However, I can guarantee you that if He does ask you to walk through it, He will be right there with you, walking alongside you. He will give you His strength, His comfort, and His peace as He does.

From Week 6 Day 4: Abuse – This is a very real thing that takes place in our world. The important thing to remember when talking about abuse is that the victim did not do anything wrong. God desires to bring healing and comfort into the wounds of abuse. I want this to be a safe place for anyone who wants to share about anything that has happened to them. We cannot fix it or erase it from having happened. But we can listen and love them and point them to God who is the Healer.

12. This day spoke into the reality of abuse. I know that this can be a very sensitive and difficult topic. Did this day's reading hit home for any of you and do you want to share anything? You only have to share if you want to.

    Give a few moments to allow anyone to share, but it is okay if no one does share.

    If anyone does share, listen. Affirm that she has been heard. Ask if you can pray for her, asking God to bring peace and comfort to her in this moment. Also pray that God will give her the wisdom to know how to keep walking forward toward healing. God has compassion toward the brokenhearted. Remind her that God sees her and His heart has compassion toward her. My prayer is that God will

Detailed Leader's Guides for All Group Meetings: Week Seven

also allow you and the other ladies' hearts in the group to also be filled with divine compassion for her and all who share this week.

From Week 6 Day 5: The importance of forgiveness –

13. Read Romans 12:14-21. Whether or not there has been abuse in our past, we have all been sinned against. How does it affect you to hear that God stands as your advocate? That He will repay?

    At times, it is easy to think that when God asks us to forgive, he is asking us to say it is okay and to sweep sin under the rug. God never says any sin is okay, whether it is my own sin or someone else's. All sin has to be paid in full. That is what Christ did on the cross.

14. Why is the cross important to remember when it comes to forgiveness?

    The cross has made forgiveness possible. The cross is the judgment, where the sin was paid in full. Forgiveness is not asking to give up justice, but to trust in God's justice, which is dealt with either on the cross or in hell. Without the cross, we could not be forgiven because justice would still be needed. When we are unwilling to forgive a fellow believer, we are saying, I know Jesus paid for it on the cross, but that wasn't enough. They owe me too.

15. Is there anyone who needs to confess bitterness before the Lord and ask God to help them forgive that person?

    It is important for us to remember that forgiveness is glorifying to God, but it is also freeing for the person who is harboring bitterness. Bitterness is one of the most destructive things to our soul. God is protecting you when He asks you to forgive. He is doing it for your well-being, and He is willing to help you do it.

16. Read Psalm 32:1-2. Spend a few minutes discussing the beauty and joy found in knowing you have been forgiven by God. With such a heavy topic this week, it would be good to end with gratitude and remembering the love and goodness of God.

CLOSING PRAYER

Make sure to spend plenty of time in prayer this evening. This may have been a very difficult discussion for some of the ladies in your group. This is a time to thank God that He cares for any pain in our past or present. He cares about how we are doing. He is also the one who can empower us to forgive others in our lives. Forgiveness is a process. Some ladies may not be ready to forgive and we do not want to judge or push them. Allow God to convict their hearts toward offering forgiveness. Be willing to pray for each of the ladies' hearts as you close.

HOMEWORK

Leave the women with a question to ponder and pose to the Lord: **"God, what is holding me back from seeking deep intimacy with You and turning over all aspects of my life to You? Please reveal it to me and give me Your strength to break free."**

> Consider writing out this assignment on separate sheets of paper for each woman in the group and handing it out at the end. Ask them to set aside five minutes this week to hear from the Lord in this way.

SELF-CRITIQUE OF MEETING

Did you encourage the women to participate, or did you dominate the time with teaching? Did each woman have enough time for sharing?

SEND A TEXT TO THE WOMEN

Make sure to send a text to each woman this week. If they shared any painful things from their past, make sure to text them thanking them for sharing and seeing how they are doing. This will help them know they have been heard. Follow-up is very important once someone has shared something painful or vulnerable about their past. Pray that God gives you the words of encouragement that you need for each lady.

MEMORY VERSE

Philippians 4:8 "Finally, brothers, whatever is true, whatever is honorable, whatever is just, whatever is pure, whatever is lovely, whatever is commendable, if there is any excellence, if there is anything worthy of praise, think about these things."

WEEK  (based on Week Seven *Study* materials)

Don't forget you are striving to cultivate healthy intimacy among the group at all times.

OPENING PRAYER

After spending some time greeting one another, open with prayer. Be willing to ask one of the other ladies if they are willing to open with prayer. This encourages them to take more ownership of the group and get even more comfortable praying in front of others. Do not be afraid to ask someone who hasn't prayed out loud yet.

SINGING

Each night, be prepared to sing one song. Be prayerful about what song to share with the ladies. It is fine if you repeat a song that you have already done. There may be one that becomes the theme song of your group.

CHECK-IN

Turn to the *Feelings Chart* in Appendix F of the *Study* and check in with how the women of the group are feeling.

> This week talked a lot about setbacks. Hopefully, it reminded them of God's grace in the midst of a setback. It also addressed the desire to stop fighting because life may have seemed easier when they were not fighting this struggle. Ask them how they are feeling when it comes to their progress and possible setbacks. Encourage them to be honest whether their emotions are feeling hopeful and

Proven Women: The Leader's Guide

encouraged or discouraged and hopeless. Allow a discussion. If there are any who seem to be discouraged, spend time in prayer over them before moving on.

CONFESSION and GOD STORIES

Allow for confession and God stories. God is always at work, and it's such a great practice to be watchful each day for ways that God is working in our lives. Let's praise God for all of the things that He has done this week. It may be empowering someone to be victorious or it may be forgiveness and cleansing for a setback. God gets the glory! He is good and at work!

DISCUSSION/TEACHING

MEMORY VERSE

Give each person a chance to recite this week's memory verse, Philippians 4:8.

Say:
- I hope you are seeing Philippians 4:8 becoming more descriptive of your mind. We have spent weeks talking about the intentionality needed to take our minds captive. We have also talked about fleeing evil and pursuing Christ. Hopefully you are seeing your mind being freed up to be able to focus on Christ and worship Him. This verse gives a great list of attributes where we should redirect our mind. How would your day be if you can say that all of your thoughts are true, honorable, just, pure, lovely, and commendable? Our minds would be so free if these words described all of our thoughts. No more jealousy, bitterness, deceit, greed, lust, etc. Like always, the things that God calls us to are both for His glory and for our well-being. Keeping our thoughts within this list is a great goal to have. But once again, we cannot do that without God's help. Anytime our thoughts go against this verse, we need to confess them before the Lord and ask Him to help us redirect toward what is good.

Ask:
- How has your thought life been this week? Are you seeing improvement since you began the *Study*?

    Give time to share.

Ask:
- If you are willing to share, what type of thoughts are the most likely to keep you from this list? Bitterness? Jealousy? Lust? Anxiety? Greed? Shame?

> Allow them to share, but also be willing to give your own answer as well.

- What do you do when you have these thoughts? Are you quick to bring them before the Lord or do you have a tendency to let them spiral?

- What can we do?

  > We have the freedom to sprint to God with these thoughts. When we confess them to the Lord, He will empower us to part with the thoughts. If we confess them as sin, He will cleanse them from us. Then we can replace the thoughts with good, life-giving thoughts. It is good to have verses on hand that we can redirect our thoughts to. Or to have worship songs that will redirect our minds to Christ.

  > Why wouldn't we want to turn to God in those moments? Bitterness, jealousy, anxiety, lust, greed, etc., are all shackles that lead us to destruction. They are miserable. Don't let them become comfortable out of familiarity. Freedom tastes so much sweeter.

Say:

When it comes to our thought life, we need to keep 2 Timothy 2:22 in mind. So flee youthful passions and pursue righteousness, faith, love, and peace along with those who call upon the Lord from a pure heart. In order to have purity of mind, there needs to be intentionality both in turning away from the negative/sinful thoughts and turning toward righteous thoughts. Look at the list in Philippians 4:8 again. These thoughts will not be available while our mind is already consumed with jealousy, bitterness or lust. We have to confess the latter for these to even be available. But, the list in Philippians 4:8 is not automatic just because our mind has become free. We need to be intentional about directing our mind toward these things. Flee and pursue! 2 Timothy 2:22 also reminds us that we are not meant to do this alone. Do this with others who call upon the Lord. Who is in your life who can help you be intentional to seek these things?

Ask:

What are the benefits in living out these verses?

  > Jealousy, greed, lust, and bitterness are destructive shackles that will control our lives. There is such joy in having our mind full of peace, love, truth, honor, etc. It truly will feel like freedom.

Proven Women: The Leader's Guide

DISCUSSION QUESTIONS FROM THE *STUDY*

You probably will not have time to discuss all of the questions, so pray through which ones you want to start with. Be willing to be flexible if the Holy Spirit steers the group in a different direction than you planned for. These questions are here to be a guide, but feel free to use your own questions as well.

From Week 7 Day 1: The voice of God, the voice of Satan, or the voice of self?

1. What are some of the differences between the two voices?

    Satan is accusing and shaming. He makes people feel like a failure or a disappointment.

    God is gracious and kind. Even His conviction over sin is meant to draw you toward Him, not to make you feel like you need to hide. God's voice will also always align with His Word. His voice will never contradict the truth of His Word. God has compassion and is never impatient.

2. Has anyone had a setback recently and wants to talk about how they felt during or after the setback?

    Satan wants us to either not care at all about a setback, or he wants us to feel like we are abandoned by God because of the setback.

    God wants us to come to Him in repentance and be restored. Remember the father in the story of the prodigal son. The father sprinted to the son and celebrated his return rather than shaming him.

From Week 7 Day 2: Read Exodus 16:1-3 and discuss.

3. The Israelites were on the road to freedom, but it was a hard road to walk. They began looking back on their slavery with rose-colored glasses. When they looked back at their slavery they described it as sitting around meat pots and eating to their fill. How is this scenario similar to someone's temptation to allow themselves to go back into their addiction to pornography?

    It's so easy to only remember the pleasure that it brought, especially when we are feeling starved for that kind of pleasure. However, looking back with those glasses is completely ignoring the fact that this was in the midst of slavery. The Israelites were in the midst of Egyptian slavery. Pornography is within the constraints of slavery to sin. Satan does not want us to remember the full picture. Just the parts you feel like you are missing. But you cannot get the pleasure without the slavery.

4. When you think back to the time when you were not fighting against your fleshly desires, what positive things may you mention? What is your version of "sat by meat pots and full of bread"?

   For some it releases stress and saying no allows stress to build up. But God never intended for us to deal with stress with sexual sin. Sex is meant only for expressions of love with our spouse. God has given other ways of dealing with stress (prayer, exercise, conversation, worship, gratitude, etc.).

   For some they will remember the pleasure of the sin fondly forgetting how they feel soon after they finish. It can never satisfy. It becomes a starving bottomless pit. But sometimes in the midst of the fight for purity, the pit is forgotten.

   It's good to identify these thoughts, so that when they pop up in your mind, you can recognize them as thoughts from Satan to lure you back to slavery.

5. Is there anything that you think pornography, masturbation, or any other sexual sin will bring you that God cannot provide?

   Remember, there is a difference between a longing and a pursuit. God may not provide the particular pursuit you are seeking, such as sexual pleasure. He will provide the longing, such as intimacy, belonging, and love.

From Week 7 Day 3: Downward spirals.

–Temptation to lust or fantasize

    –Acting out

        –Feeling guilty

            –Experiencing shame or self-condemnation

                –Turning inward (shutting out friends and community)

                    –Desiring to escape

                        –Temptation to lust or fantasize

6. How have you seen this cycle in your life?

7. What is a recurring lie Satan may use to trip you up into this cycle?

   If someone acts out and they experience conviction, they can break this cycle by turning to God in repentance rather than turning inward and shutting everyone out, including God. Repentance rescues us from the need to escape because rather than feeling humiliating shame, we can have gratitude and awe over the amazing grace of God. Rather than fleeing from the presence of God, we can come boldly before His throne to receive mercy in time of need and worship Him for His righteousness, His loving kindness, and His graciousness.

8. We need to replace our negative, deceitful, or evil thoughts with truthful thoughts. What are some things you have been dwelling on lately, good or bad?

9. How are you being intentional with your thoughts? If you are not, how should you start being intentional with your thoughts?

From Week 7 Day 4:

10. Read Jeremiah 18:1-4 and discuss.

11. How are you allowing God to reshape you?

12. Describe some of the patterns of this world to which you still conform.

> TV shows that glorify sex, comparing yourself to other women in appearance or skill, materialism, jealousy, judgmental attitudes, remaining in a relationship you know God is calling you out of.

From Week 7 Day 5: Meditation with the Lord.

13. I hope this day provided a very special time for you to be with the Lord. Does anyone want to share about that time? It is good to share God stories, because it is praising God for what He has done. Does anyone want to share?

> Be willing to share about yours if no one opens up at first.

PRAYER

Stand holding hands in a circle. Go around the circle having each woman pray. You can start or end.

HOMEWORK

Tell the women:
- Next week is going to encourage you to do some sort of fast. It is not required for anyone, but I want you to seriously pray about doing some sort of fast. You will also be asked to fast from social media and all other media. We are all a team and we will be doing it

together. We can encourage one another throughout the week to remain steadfast as we fight our fleshly desires.

SELF-CRITIQUE

After the meeting, conduct a self-evaluation of the meeting. Did you allow for full discussion? Did each woman participate? Make an effort to draw out those who are less participatory, with questions such as, "How did that make you feel?" "Can you describe it in more detail?" or "What did you do next?" or by using other open-ended questions.

SEND A TEXT TO THE WOMEN

I'm very proud of your commitment to the group and your commitment to sexual integrity. Keep at it. Remember we are on this journey together. I'm here for you and I'm praying for you.

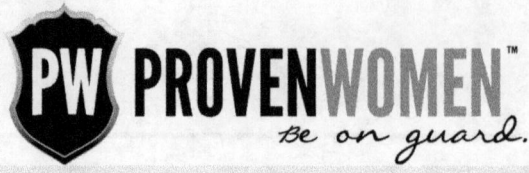

Passionate for God,
Repentant in spirit,
Open and honest,
Victorious in living,
Eternal in perspective, and
Networking with other *Proven Women.*

MEMORY VERSE

Psalm 19:13-14 "Keep back your servant also from presumptuous sins; let them not have dominion over me! Then I shall be blameless, and innocent of great transgression. Let the words of my mouth and the meditation of my heart be acceptable in your sight, O Lord, my rock and my redeemer."

WEEK  (based on Week Eight *Study* materials)

OPENING PRAYER

Make sure to open the time with prayer after allowing the ladies some time to interact and catch up.

SINGING

Each night, be prepared to sing one song. As always, be prayerful about what song to sing with the group. You are welcome to have a new song each week or to have discovered one that has become a theme song for your group and use that same song each week.

CHECK-IN

Turn to the *Feelings Chart* in Appendix F of the *Study* and ask each woman to check in with how they are feeling and how they felt during the week. This past week, the ladies were invited to participate in a fast. This may have amplified some of their emotions this past week. They may have experienced unusual amounts of irritability or discouragement. Or they may have experienced more hope and feelings of encouragement. Remind them of the importance of honesty. Do not simply state the positive emotions while ignoring the negative. Honesty helps address and process these emotions. Denying negative emotions does not change the reality that they existed throughout the week. It is best to be aware of them so that they can be acknowledged in community and to the Lord. He is the one who can transform the heart and mind.

Proven Women: The Leader's Guide

CONFESSION and GOD STORIES

Hopefully everyone is becoming more adept at spotting God at work in their lives. It is such a beautiful thing to have our God-radar on and to celebrate the things He has done by sharing them with others. Also, hopefully our hearts continue to break over the sin in our lives, yet we celebrate the peace that comes from repentance and cleansing. Praise God for His grace.

DISCUSSION/TEACHING

State:
- This week, we were asked to fast. Like it said in the *Study,* fasting isn't a magic formula to help you get quicker results, but it can help you focus more on God and learn more self-discipline. Does anyone want to share about how the fast went for you?

    > Be willing to share about your week and your fast if no one else opens up. Some truly discover breakthrough because there is power in fasting. Remember not to shame anyone if they did not fast or tried to fast and failed. But do remind them that God calls us to fast for a reason. There truly is power in humbling ourselves before God through fasting. Encourage them to try again the following week if they did not this week, but the choice is theirs.

State:
- This week, we were also asked to give up social media and television. Sometimes we do not realize how much these are impacting our lives until we cut them out completely. Does anyone want to share about how cutting out media affected their week?

    > Once again, be willing to share first.

State:
- As we have been going through the *Proven Women Study,* I hope you are becoming more aware of the things that are going on within your heart. We have learned that our hearts are often selfish and prideful. We have also learned that it is important for us to be willing to work through deep pain that we have experienced. Some of this pain could be from unmet desires and expectations. Some of this pain could be from how we have been treated over the years. It is so tempting to avoid and escape the pain in our hearts. But God does not simply want escape, He wants freedom for us. Escape is temporary. Freedom will be lasting because it comes through healing.

- One of the effects of fasting is that it takes away some of the things that we may be using to escape mentalities or emotions God desires to address. By cutting out possible hours of mindless television and social media, there was probably time this week for thoughts and feelings to surface that usually stay under the surface. God wants to know these thoughts. If they are sinful, He is the One who can cleanse and forgive them. If they are painful, He is the One who can comfort and heal. If they are lies, He is the One who can transform them into truth. Rather than burying, ignoring, or avoiding the things within our heart, it is so crucial to our walk with the Lord to bring our true thoughts and motives before the Lord in humility, acknowledging if/when they are wrong, but still acknowledging them.

- 1 Peter 5: "Cast all of your anxieties on Him because He cares for you." Let's never forget that God cares. He has such compassion for each of us. We can trust Him with our heart.

This is a great transition into our memory verse because our memory verse speaks of the thoughts and intentions of our heart.

MEMORY VERSE

Ask someone to recite this week's memory verse, Psalm 19:13-14.

Now Read Psalm 19:7-14.

Ask:

According to these verses, what can we expect the Word of God to do for us?
- Revive the soul
- Make wise the simple
- Enlighten the eyes
- Rejoice the heart
- Be more desirable than the choicest of food
- Bring warning and also great reward in keeping them

Ask:

Do we truly believe that the Scriptures can do each of these things for our heart and mind? What are your thoughts on this passage?

State:

Do we see that spending time in God's Word helps us to have pure thoughts and intentions before the Lord? Let's say that I am being honest with God about my true thoughts and feelings. Some of those thoughts are really selfish and sinful. If I am not in God's Word, I may not recognize them as selfish and see the need to repent. This is why both prayer and Bible reading are important together. It is the process of expressing our heart while also having in mind the lens of Scripture that allows God to transform and heal our heart. We need to see our heart against the backdrop of truth.

Ask:

How has your view of Scripture grown or changed throughout these eight weeks?

> Allow a couple of minutes for discussion.

DISCUSSION QUESTIONS FROM THE *STUDY*

From Week 8 Day 1:

1. We already discussed how the actual fast went this past week, but how do you think the fast affected your walk with the Lord and this fight against lust?

2. Pride and selfishness are the root causes of a lack of intimacy and a consequent turning toward sexual immorality. In your own words, describe how selfishness and pride can keep sexual sins alive in someone's life.

   > Pride can keep people from repenting or going to God for help. Selfishness can keep us from desiring to obey God. If we allow selfishness to continue to rule our life, we will want to follow our own fleshly desires more than we will want to honor God with our life.

3. Did you make a list of issues and conversations you needed to address? Were you able to address these?

   > Be willing to share your own if God put something on your heart as well.

From Week 8 Day 2:

4. List ways in which you are powerless today (e.g., addiction, controlling boss or spouse, debt, deadlines, overwhelming fear). How do you feel in times of powerlessness?

5. How has the need for control in different areas of your life kept you from trusting God's way for your life and turning to God for the intimacy that you need? Or, how have you chosen to turn to God while relinquishing control?

6. Why is it tempting to turn to different outlets of lust rather than true intimacy?

7. How is relinquishing control to God better than clinging to control in our life?

   > God always knows better. He is the one who is powerful. He is loving and good. He always does things with pure motives. He is so much wiser and more trustworthy than we are. And He does care!

From Week 8 Day 3:

8. Even after being in this *Study* for so many weeks and hearing about our need to rely on God over and over, it is still tempting to try to do this on our own. List some ways in which you have been performance-based this week.

   Remind them that we do not ask these questions to condemn anyone. We want to bring these mental tendencies to light so that we can fight against them. God longs to lead us to freedom. So many times our thoughts and desires can get in the way. If we leave them alone, they begin to rule over us again. When we constantly bring them before the Lord and each other, we are recognizing them as destructive and we work together to fight against them.

9. Read Matthew 7:24-29 and discuss the difference between the wise and the foolish man.

   The wise man doesn't just hear God's Word, but also puts it into practice. The foolish man hears it but does not act on it.

10. How are you guys doing? We are eight weeks in and it has asked a LOT of you. Are you putting into practice the things that you are reading and hearing?

    Give them a few minutes to discuss.

From Week 8 Day 4:

11. Day Four talked about overcoming shame-based thinking. Does anyone want to share any commitments you are making to overcome shame-based thinking?

From Week 8 Day 5:

12. Day Five talks about selfishness even in our relationship with the Lord and with our spouse (friends). How can we be selfish with the Lord?

    We go to Him for what He can do for us rather than going to Him to love and worship Him. We focus more on His hand, what He is doing, than we do on seeking His face. We picture Him as a genie in the sky or a benevolent grandpa rather than the Almighty God who is worthy of our worship.

    How can we be selfish with our spouse (friends)?

    We seek the pleasure they will bring us rather than loving them. We seek how they will fulfill our emotional needs rather than putting their interests before our own, like it says in Philippians 2. Of course, as we love our husbands or friends if we are single, many times we experience pleasure as they meet some of our emotional needs. That is good. But when our focus is selfishness, we feel entitled to please ourselves when they fall short.

13. Read Psalm 51 and discuss.

14. The last part of Day Five spoke a lot about repentance. Does anyone want to share anything that God did in your heart in this portion of the homework?

PRAYER

As you get ready for prayer, ask the women:

- Have you finally agreed to give up complete control of every aspect of your life?

For prayer time, ask the women to lie face down with their arms stretched out.

> It will be a bit intimidating, so get on your knees and start lying down. Explain that we are to be needy, dependent servants, and that you are using this posture to help you pour your heart out to the Lord. Ask the women to do the same, and as you each get into position, tell the women to open their hearts to God and to confess any sins or make commitments to the Lord. Be a good example by praying a short, heartfelt petition, confessing some sin and pledging to put down the shovel or similar words as found in Psalm 51 or Galatians 2:20. Give each woman time to pray while on their knees.

HOMEWORK

Continue to encourage the ladies to set aside thirty to forty-five minutes each day for the *Study*. Encourage them to remain diligent and steadfast in their pursuit of the Holy Spirit daily.

Ask the ladies to set aside five minutes sometime this week to hear from the Lord as to what area(s) in your life you are still controlling. (PRINT THE STEPS BELOW FOR EACH WOMAN OR HAVE THEM WRITE DOWN THE STEPS.)

1. Still your heart and find a quiet place to meet with the Lord, preparing yourself for asking Him to reveal what areas you are still controlling or refusing to turn over to Him.

2. With a blank sheet of paper (or in your journal), earnestly ask God: **"What am I holding on to?"**

3. Simply jot down any rough thoughts or flashes as they enter your mind. Do not dwell on any one item at this time, but just keep jotting down a word or two at a time. Keep asking the Lord if there is any other area, and simply write down anything that enters your mind.

4. After several minutes of asking and seeking the Lord, go back to the sheet and read what you wrote down. Now ask the Lord to open your heart as you read each item. God will make it clear to you whether they were your own thoughts or Him speaking to you.

5. Review the points about which you believe God was speaking to you. Ask Him to reveal more of how you have been holding on to these areas or acting in pride or selfishness. Talk to Him about it.

6. Decide that you will respond and do whatever the Lord is asking you. Commit to act upon what God reveals to you. Don't hold back or fight the Holy Spirit by glossing over an item.

7. Prepare a plan for action. (Be a doer, not just a hearer—James 1:22.)

SELF-CRITIQUE

Did you allow for full discussion? Did each woman participate? Make an effort to draw out those who are more quiet, with questions such as, "So, how did that make you feel?" "Can you describe it in more detail?" or "What did you do next?" or by using other open-ended questions?

SEND A TEXT TO THE WOMEN

Remember, a relationship with the Lord is one of constant growth. It may be helpful to go back through the material with a heart desiring to know God even better, and it may also be beneficial to consider repeating the entire *Study* at the end of the twelve weeks. The second time through the *Study* will be fresh and exciting as God reveals Himself even more. Keep at it.

Passionate for God,
Repentant in spirit,
Open and honest,
Victorious in living,
Eternal in perspective, and
Networking with other *Proven Women.*

MEMORY VERSE

2 Corinthians 10:5 "We demolish arguments and every pretension that sets itself up against the knowledge of God, and we take captive every thought to make it obedient to Christ."

WEEK  (based on Week Nine *Study* materials)

OPENING PRAYER

After spending some time greeting one another, open with prayer. Use this as a time to invite Christ into the group and allow His Spirit to lead the discussion.

SINGING

Each night, be prepared to sing one song. Hopefully this has become a very sweet time of worship for the ladies as a group.

CHECK-IN

Turn to the *Feelings Chart* in Appendix F of the *Study* and check in with how everyone is feeling and how their week went. Hopefully by now this is a very natural part of the group. Pray that the girls continue to be honest and open about how their week has been and how they are currently doing tonight.

GOD STORIES and CONFESSION

Spend some time discussing how their fight against lust went throughout the week. Make sure to share both about how God had been at work as well as confess any fallbacks. As people confess, remind them of 1 John 1:9, "If we confess our sin, He is faithful and just to forgive us of all sin and cleanse us of all unrighteousness." Also, remind them of Jesus' response to the woman who had been caught in adultery. "Neither do I condemn you, but go and sin no

Proven Women: The Leader's Guide

more." It is such a beautiful thing that God does not condemn us because of the cross. But we need to also remember that God wants us to walk away from sin and pursue righteousness.

DISCUSSION/TEACHING

MEMORY VERSE

Ask someone to recite the memory verse, 2 Corinthians 10:5.

Ask:
- What is this verse calling us to do? How have you been able to put this verse into practice this week?

  > The battle often starts in the mind. This verse is calling us to obey Christ at the thought level; taking captive our thoughts to the obedience of Christ. This can mean lustful, selfish, or other sinful thoughts. This could also mean being diligent in taking captive our thoughts when we think something that we know is not true about God. Perhaps you had a nagging thought this week that God doesn't care about you. We have to recognize these thoughts as wrongful thinking and take them captive. It is better for us to be in control of our thoughts than for our thoughts to control us.

State:
- We have now been going through this study for nine weeks. The purpose of this study is both to help you find freedom from sexual sin and to cultivate your relationship with God. Let's spend some time this week talking about how this study has impacted our view of who God is. In this study, we were asked, "Do I believe God is good? Do I trust God with total control over all areas of my life?"
- No matter how much we do believe God is good, I know we can always continue to grow even more in this belief. Because if all of us believed 100 percent with all of our heart that God is good and we were trusting Him, we would not be turning to anything else. We would be perfect. There is still room for growth, but I am confident that each of us has grown in our trust in God throughout this study. Does anyone want to share what they have learned about God through this study?

  > Give time for the ladies to share. Be willing to share yourself. Also, be affirming to each of the ones who did share. Let them know how proud you are of the work and time they are investing in this study. Praise God that He is revealing so much to your group.

State:
- Also, you may have noticed that the Bible reading was a little different this week. Usually, we read a chapter that pertains to the lesson. For the next few weeks, we will be reading through whole books of the Bible. This is getting you into the practice of Bible reading so that you will hopefully continue this practice once the group is over. So each week we will also talk about the Bible reading as well.

DISCUSSION QUESTIONS FROM THE *STUDY*

Read through the questions ahead of time and pray through which ones you should ask during the group. Be familiar with the questions so that you can segue into a new question out of order if the discussion happens to go in a different direction. As always, do not feel pressure to ask all of the questions. Always ask if there was any part of the *Study* that the girls wanted to discuss or anything that stood out to them.

From Week 9 Day 1:

1. This week asked us to take some serious action if we are still dabbling in sexual sin. It called us to examine our heart and ask if we truly saw it as evil. It also called us to destroy things that still may be tempting us.

   Did anyone destroy or remove anything from their home or phone this week?

From Week 9 Day 2:

2. In Day Two, the *Study* compared pornography to an idol. It called an idol, "anything you greatly admire or pursue instead of the Lord." Colossians 3:5-6 "Put to death, therefore, whatever belongs to your earthly nature: Sexual immorality, impurity, lust, evil desires and greed, which is idolatry. Because of these, the wrath of God is coming."

   Describe how looking at pornography or looking at another person with lust in your heart is the same as making pornography or self-gratification an idol in your life.

   > Looking at pornography is choosing something other than God to fulfill the longing of your heart. Not only is it something other than God, it is the very thing that He has called us not to set our heart toward.

3. Explain in your own words why spending more time with God and worshiping Him are the antidotes for lust and impurity.

   > Worshiping God is acknowledging how great and awesome God is and expressing that admiration to God. Gratitude and praise flow out of the heart. There is nothing selfish about expressing praise and worship to God. Lust is all about one's own

gratification and selfishness. Spending time with God will allow you to get your heart off of yourself and onto God.

From Week 9 Day 3:

4. Once again, our memory verse is 2 Corinthians 10:5. Who can restate it in their own words?

5. What type of thoughts should we be taking captive?

    Obviously sexual lust, since that is what this group is about, but let's not stop there. We should take captive jealous thoughts, slanderous thoughts, bitter thoughts, judgmental thoughts. Sometimes, we may be tempted to think all of our thoughts are fine as long as we do not voice the thoughts or act on them. But these thoughts begin to control our mind. It is hard to be kind to someone when we allow ourselves to slander them in our mind. It is hard to be jealous and worshipful at the same time.

6. How can the PROVEN acrostic help us with our thoughts?

    P – our thoughts should be fueled by our passion for the Lord.

    R – when we have evil thoughts, we should repent.

    O – we should be open and honest even about our thoughts within our group so that we can pray for one another and hold one another accountable in this group.

    V – we will be victorious with our thoughts when we take them captive and redirect them toward the things listed in Philippians 4:8.

    E – having an eternal perspective will also help us keep our thoughts focused on what is good rather than instant gratification.

    N – we are not meant to do this alone, but with other sisters in Christ.

From Week 9 Day 4:

7. As we talk about setbacks this week, it is also important to talk about how we feel after we commit a sin. Describe how you feel after you cave in to some sort of sexual sin.

    Most times there is shame and failure. It is true that God will forgive us and cleanse us, but the conviction is very real. We should think about this before we allow ourselves to cave in.

8. Many singles who struggle with masturbation or pornography think the temptation will go away once they get married because they will be able to have sex with their husband at that point. Why is marriage not the fix-all for sexual sin?

   Sexual sin is all about self-gratification. Marriage is about selflessness and love. When you see masturbation and pornography as an option before marriage, it will be an option when your husband isn't living up to your expectations. Plus, since you have been pleasing yourself for so long, it will be hard for him to live up to your expectations. No one can compete with a fantasy.

   Sexual sin has pride and selfishness at its core. A wedding does not change your heart from pride to humility. The heart needs to change, not just the actions.

9. Read James 1:13-15 and discuss what causes temptations.

   Our own desires. This is why the heart needs to change, not just the actions.

From Week 9 Day 5:

10. When you draw a line and decide that masturbation and pornography or any other sexual sin is not an option, expect a battle. Sometimes the urge gets even stronger. How has the battle against sexual sin been this week?

11. How can we be selfish with the Lord?

    We go to Him for what He can do for us rather than going to Him to love and worship Him. We focus more on His hand, what He is doing, than we do on seeking His face.

12. How can we be selfish with our spouse (friends)?

    We seek the pleasure they will bring us rather than loving them. We seek how they will fulfill our emotional needs rather than putting their interests before our own like it says in Philippians 2. Of course, as we love our husbands or friends if we are single, many times we experience pleasure as they meet some of our emotional needs. That is good. But when our focus is selfishness, we feel entitled to please ourselves when they fall short.

13. Read Psalm 51 and discuss.

14. The last part of Day Five spoke a lot about repentance. Does anyone want to share anything that God did in your heart in this portion of the homework?

1 PETER

This week, you read through 1 Peter. Is there anything that you learned about God this week from the Bible reading? Anything that was encouraging? Anything that was convicting?

Insights from 1 Peter

(1:13) "Therefore, preparing your minds for action, be sober-minded, set your hope fully on the grace that will be brought to you at the revelation of Jesus Christ." *Here is another call to be intentional with our mind.*

(2:1) "So put away all malice and all deceit and hypocrisy and envy and all slander." *This is a list of more issues of the heart that Peter is calling us to fight against.*

(2:9) "But you are a chosen race, a royal priesthood, a holy nation, a people for his own possession, that you may proclaim the excellencies of him who called you out of darkness and into his marvelous light." *When we feel unworthy, remember the truth of who He says you are. And He does it so that you can proclaim Him as excellent.*

(3:1-6) – *These verses talk about wives and husbands. It also defines beauty for us. What do you think it means that beauty is a gentle and quiet spirit? Gentle and quiet spirit does not mean how loud a person is. A gentle and quiet spirit is a woman who knows who she is in Christ. She walks into a room to love others, not to gain affirmation from others. She may engage others with many words or a peaceful quiet. It is not about her volume but rather about her ability to love others well.*

Chapter 4 reminds us that there will be suffering in this life, but Christ has also suffered with us and for us. He understands our suffering and will empower you as you go through it.

(5:6-9) Be humble, cast your anxieties on God because He cares, resist the devil—he is trying to destroy you.

PRAYER

Spend the last fifteen minutes in prayer. Give each woman an opportunity to pour out her heart to the Lord and make commitments.

HOMEWORK

Encourage everyone to continue the *Study* daily and purpose to keep meeting with the Lord instead of just doing homework.

SELF-CRITIQUE

Did you allow for full discussion? Did each woman participate? Did you make an effort to draw out those who are more quiet with open-ended questions?

SEND A TEXT TO THE WOMEN

I am praying for you. Keep an eternal perspective. Never forget how much Jesus loves you. He also gives grace to you when you are humble (James 4:6). Therefore, commit in your heart to become a needy, dependent servant of Christ.

Passionate for God,
Repentant in spirit,
Open and honest,
Victorious in living,
Eternal in perspective, and
Networking with other *Proven Women.*

MEMORY VERSE

Ephesians 6:12: "For we do not wrestle against flesh and blood, but against the rulers, against the authorities, against the cosmic powers over this present darkness, against the spiritual forces of evil in the heavenly places.'"

WEEK  11 (based on Week Ten *Study* materials)

OPENING PRAYER

Spend the first several minutes opening in prayer.

SINGING

Each night, be prepared to sing one song together as a group. Let this be a song that exalts Christ.

CHECK-IN

Turn to the *Feelings Chart* in Appendix F of the *Study* and spend time allowing each woman to share about their week and how they are doing. If they bring up an incident, have them share how they were feeling before it, during it, immediately after the incident. Ask if they went to the Lord about the incident and how they felt after engaging with the Lord.

GOD STORIES and CONFESSION

Continue to celebrate God stories/victories and also give them opportunity for confession if there were any setbacks.

Proven Women: The Leader's Guide

DISCUSSION/TEACHING

MEMORY VERSE

Ask someone to recite the memory verse, Ephesians 6:12.

After you recite or read the memory verse, ask someone if they can paraphrase it in their own words. Then ask how the memory verse has encouraged them this week.

> It is helpful to remember that the only true enemy that we have is Satan. People are not our enemy. We do not wrestle against flesh and blood—people—but we do wrestle. That wrestling is against spiritual warfare. This is a reminder that we need to resist Satan and lean into Christ.

Ask:

- How would it change our perspective if we truly saw Satan as the enemy, rather than the people in our life whom God has called us to love and forgive?

State:

- We have been focusing on cultivating our walk with the Lord while walking toward purity. We have also addressed how all temptation comes from our own desires. Galatians 5:16-26 brings this all together for us.

    > Read Galatians 5:16-26.

State:

- Look at the list in verses 19-21. We have spent much of our time talking about sexual sin, but let's list the ones in these verses that are not sexual.

    > Idolatry, sorcery, strife, jealousy, fits of anger, rivalry, dissention, division, drunkenness.

- God is calling us to holiness, and that should include every area of our life. We have been very focused on dealing with the sexual sin in our life. Let us also be as adamant about the other sins in our life as well. God desires to free us from all works of unrighteousness. We do this by repenting of our sin and asking Him to transform our life. We invite God to help us. We trust God to forgive and cleanse us of these things as we repent of them (1 John 1:9).

- Now look at the list in verses 22–23. This is the fruit that God desires to bring into our life, and He will as we rely on the Spirit.

- As we reflect on this past week, do we see more works of the flesh or more fruit of the Spirit? We do not ask this to condemn anyone. We ask to bring hope. God's fruit is available to anyone who is walking in His Spirit. No matter how this past week was, we can have hope for this next week.

    Give them time to share their thoughts.

DISCUSSION QUESTIONS FROM THE *STUDY*

Remember to go through the questions beforehand. You may not have time to go through them all and that is okay. Ask the Lord to lead the discussion. Be sure to allow the girls to share anything from the *Study* that stood out to them even if it is not in the questions.

From Week 10 Day 1:

1. How can you say with your lips, "God, free me from masturbation," if your heart is also saying, "But I don't really want to meet with you personally or daily?" What pride it takes to say, "Heal me of pornography" but to then keep God at bay because you think you can provide for yourself in other areas? Why should there be a connection between overcoming sin and also desiring to spend time with God and relying on Him?

    God designed us for intimacy with Him. We should not be doing this study just to find freedom from sin. Our goal is not to overcome this addiction just for freedom's sake so that we can be free to do whatever we want. The purpose is to free our heart to be more inclined to worship and love God. To grow in intimacy with God, we need to direct ourselves not only away from sin, but we should be redirecting toward God.

2. Here's a helpful question to determine whether and why a person is still in bondage to sexual sins: "Am I willing to do whatever it takes to receive God's healing?" Can you honestly say, "No matter what the cost, Lord, I am willing"? How are you all doing with these questions?

From Week 10 Day 2:

3. Read Matthew 6:24. "No one can serve two masters, for either he will hate the one and love the other, or he will be devoted to the one and despise the other. You cannot serve God and money." Day Two talked about contentment. Why can nobody serve both God and money/other selfish pleasures?

    The Lord knows that the love of money (greed or pursuing material things) keeps you from being content with what He knows is best for you. Your desire for temporary selfish pleasures will only drag you away from God's camp and

Proven Women: The Leader's Guide

    breed discontentment. Is God's love enough for you? Will you be content with Him alone?

4. "If you spend time with Jesus with the goal of getting to know Him, you'll fall in love with Him. Then, you'll want what Christ wants more than you will want sexually immoral activities." How have you seen this played out in your life over the past weeks?

From Week 10 Day 3:

5. I know this is a hard question to ask for those whose answer is "yes," but I hope everyone knows this is a safe place. Do any of you fear aspects of intimacy, i.e., letting your guard down or being completely open with someone? Explain why.

6. This week we were asked to commit to a lifestyle of worship and praise. Does anyone want to share how they are putting this into practice?

7. Pride makes us think we can do this on our own. Why does self-sufficient thinking keep us from God? Why is this thinking so tempting?

> Some really feel the need to do this on their own. They don't think they deserve God's help or they were taught by their family they had to be strong and fend for themselves. Some want to please God with their actions on their own rather than needing God. Some fear that God will let them down and feel the need to cling to control in their own life. The problem is we cannot do this without God. It does not please Him to attempt to do this in our strength. He never intended for us to live righteously without Him. We are meant to be in constant relationship with Him. The relationship is more important than the behavior to God. The good news is a true, intimate relationship with Christ will result in transformed behavior.

From Week 10 Day 4:

8. Day Four speaks of spiritual warfare. Pick a few of the following verses to read with the ladies in your group: Matthew 4:1, John 8:44, Ephesians 6:12, Matthew 13:19, John 12:31, Matthew 4:3.

   What are a few things that stand out to you about Satan either from these verses or the daily reading?

   > He is the tempter, a murderer, the father of lies, he is a roaring lion. He seeks to destroy. He does not play nice. He will kick you while you are down.

9. Read Ephesians 4:26-27. "Be angry and do not sin, do not let the sun go down on your anger, and give no opportunity to the devil." According to this verse, what gives opportunity to the devil?

Anger... however, this can also refer to any unconfessed internal sin. Jealousy, bitterness, greed. When we allow these things to remain in our heart and mind, we give Satan an open door into our life. He will use these to wreak havoc in our lives and relationships.

10. What is the good news of James 4:7-8?

    When we stand with God and resist Satan, he will flee from us. But notice that it takes intentionality to submit to God and resist Satan. This is a steadfastness that must be developed by spending time with God often. When we stand with Christ, Satan will be defeated in that moment.

11. Read Ephesians 6:10-18.

    Use the appendix in the back of the *Study* to describe each of the pieces of armor.

12. Why do we need armor?

    Because we are in a spiritual battle, and these are the things God created to fight well within this battle. Remember it is not the pieces of armor that are important but what they represent. Rather than focus on shield, focus on faith. Our weapons are salvation, righteousness, faith, Scripture, truth, prayer, and peace.

From Week 10 Day 5:

13. The last day was a day of reflection and meditation. Does anyone want to share anything that they gleaned from this day?

    Be willing to share from your own experience.

EPHESIANS

This past week, we also read through the book of Ephesians. Does anyone want to share anything that stood out from the reading of Ephesians? Anything that was encouraging? Anything that was convicting? (These insights below are for you to use in the discussion if they would be helpful to you and if you have time.) Feel free to just let the ladies discuss what they got out of their reading. This does not need to be an additional teaching time, but a time of discussion if time allows.

Insights from Ephesians

(1:3-14) Paul walks through the blessing of being a Christian. He mentions that we are blessed with every spiritual blessing, loved by God, chosen and adopted beloved daughters, and so much more. All of this was done through the glorious grace of Christ. It is because of Christ's obedience and sacrifice that we have been granted this inheritance.

(1:15-23) Paul writes out a prayer for spiritual wisdom for those to whom he is writing this letter. This prayer is a model for ways we can be praying for one another.

(2:1-10) We were dead in our sins and children of God's wrath, but God. "But God"—such beautiful words. This passage reminds us that our salvation is not because of anything that we have done. It is because of God's grace and mercy that He saved us. We do not deserve it and we were spiritually dead. But placing faith in Christ makes us alive with Christ.

(2:11-22) Christ's death and resurrection should bring unity to the church. There is no division between Jew and Gentile. There should be no division based on race, gender, or other issues that often cause division. Jesus has made all believers one in Him. That should remind us also that God does not see any one of us as an outsider. He has made us one with Christ and with others of the church. Each of us is a citizen with God's holy people. Each of us belong.

(3:14-21) Another beautiful prayer which Paul wrote. He prayed that we would be rooted in Christ's love and comprehend how wide, high, long, and deep is that love. He also reminds us that God can do immeasurably more than we could ever ask or imagine, but He does it all for HIS glory.

(4:11-16) God has called certain people to equip the saints for the work of the ministry. Notice that all of the saints are called to the work of the ministry. God's desire is for His people to be built up in maturity so that each man and woman is grounded in doctrine and not thrown around by the opinions of the world.

(4:17-32) The difference between the old life and the new life in Christ.

Chapter 5 continues the talk of how walking in love and the light should play out. We are to put away things of darkness. It also includes how this should affect the roles within the home. Husbands and wives. All should be done in love and humility.

(6:1-9) Paul continues to speak to certain roles. Children, parents, masters, servants. These are at the end of the book because we rely on the truth written earlier in the book in order to live this out. We are walking in the love of Christ. He knows we are redeemed and loved by God. It is because of this, we can love one another well.

(6:10-24) Armor of God and Spiritual Warfare.

Detailed Leader's Guides for All Group Meetings: Week Eleven

PRAYER

For prayer time, pray for God to equip each woman with the Armor of God this week. Remember, do not just pray for the piece of armor but also what it represents—not just shield, but shield of Faith!

HOMEWORK

Ask the women to meditate on Galatians 5:16-26 throughout the coming week and to commit to journaling about it. Ask them to commit to the decision that sexual sin is no longer an option.

SELF-CRITIQUE

Did you allow for full discussion? Did each woman participate? Make an effort to draw out those who are less participatory.

SEND A TEXT TO THE WOMEN

Victory is found by spending time with God in prayer and praise, reading the Bible (which melts your heart and resets your eternal perspective button), being open and honest with your feelings, networking with others, and basically taking on all six of the letters in the *PROVEN* acrostic.

> **P** is for Passionate for God,
>
> **R** is for Repentant in spirit,
>
> **O** is for Open and honest,
>
> **V** is for Victorious in living,
>
> **E** is for Eternal in perspective, and
>
> **N** is for Networking with other *PROVEN Women*.

That's why the by-product of intimacy with God is the loosening of the grip of sexual sin! That's also why the goal of knowing Jesus is the cure and why a goal of stopping a certain sin won't result in victory.

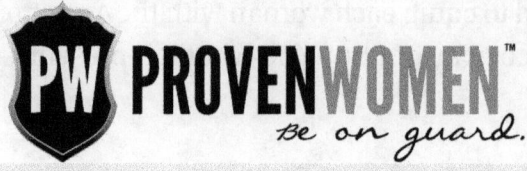

Passionate for God,
Repentant in spirit,
Open and honest,
Victorious in living,
Eternal in perspective, and
Networking with other *Proven Women.*

MEMORY VERSE

Ephesians 4:1-2 "I therefore, a prisoner for the Lord, urge you to walk in a manner worthy of the calling to which you have been called, with all humility and gentleness, with patience, bearing with one another in love."

WEEK  12 (based on Week Eleven *Study* materials)

OPENING PRAYER

After spending some time greeting one another, open with prayer, inviting God to join the group and dedicating the time to Him.

SINGING

Each night, be prepared to sing one song. Feel free to use the same song each week as a theme song if you have gone that route. If not, choose a song this week that encourages the women to live for the Lord and to surrender their entire heart to Him.

CHECK-IN

Turn to the *Feelings Chart* in Appendix F of the *Study* and check in with how everyone is feeling. Be sure to ask how they are doing this evening, but also throughout the week. Be willing to stop and pray for anyone who seems to need it.

GOD STORIES and CONFESSION

This section is crucial for healing. Please continue to celebrate God stories/victories and allow time for them to confess any setbacks throughout the week. Always remind them of the beauty of God's grace and forgiveness, yet His desire that we go and sin no more. Ask God to give you the wisdom to know how to encourage someone who is still having setbacks each week.

Proven Women: The Leader's Guide

DISCUSSION/TEACHING

MEMORY VERSE

Ask someone to recite the Memory Verse, Ephesians 4:1-2.

Ask:
- How has this memory verse impacted your life this week?

    Give them time to share.

Say:
- When Paul says that he is a prisoner for the Lord, he is not being symbolic or using a metaphor. He is wearing literal chains for the sake of the gospel. And he is calling people to walk in a manner worthy of the calling to which they have been called. He is not calling them to be worthy of the gospel. The gospel has made us worthy. The gospel has given us this calling. In chapter 1 of Ephesians we see that God chose us before the foundation of the world, that we should be holy and blameless. We have been adopted as daughters. God has redeemed and forgiven us. Now Paul is asking us to step into that calling. Verse 2 of our memory verses tells us how to walk worthy—with all humility and gentleness, with patience, bearing with one another in love. We walk worthy of our call when we walk in humility, gentleness, patience, and love. Notice that besides humility, the rest of these are fruits of the Spirit.

Ask:
- What is humility?
    - *Humility is understanding your need for God. Rather than trying to prove ourselves to God, it is understanding that without God, we will continue to fall and fail. Humility is also putting the interests of others before our own (Philippians 2:3-4).*
    - *A couple other thoughts about humility: Humility is not thinking lowly about oneself but simply not thinking about oneself. Humility is similar to selflessness or self-forgetfulness. This type of humility takes confidence in God's love for us and His power and strength. Humility is not a disregard or hatred for oneself. It does not mean that you do not care about yourself, but you have such a focus on the love of God, grace of God, provision of God, wisdom of God, that you look to Him rather than fending for oneself. And there is such love for others that it becomes natural to put their interests before your own.*

Ask:
- Why do you think humility is listed first in verse 2?

Detailed Leader's Guides for All Group Meetings: Week Twelve

- *It takes humility for us to realize that we cannot do this on our own. We have to humble ourselves before the Lord and choose to walk in the Spirit in order to see the fruit of the Spirit. By walking in the Spirit, we will walk worthy of our calling. And it is only through the Spirit that we will do this. Our love for others will be evident as we walk with our Lord.*

Ask:

How have you seen Ephesians 4:1-2 develop in your life over the past eleven weeks? Do you believe that you are walking more worthy of your calling now than before? What has made this difference? Where do you still need to surrender to the Lord?

DISCUSSION QUESTIONS FROM THE *STUDY*

You probably will not have time to discuss all of the questions, so pray through which ones you want to start with. Be willing to be flexible if the Holy Spirit steers the group in a different direction than you planned. These questions are here to be a guide, but feel free to use your own questions as well.

From Week 11 Day 1:

1. Read 1 John 2:15-17 and discuss. What is your initial response when you hear these verses?

    It's important to define our words. When John says to not love the world, he is referring to the lust of the flesh, the lust of the eyes, and the pride of life. He is referring to all of the works of the flesh in Galatians 5:19-21. He is not talking about the earth (creation) or people. But we should be repulsed by the evil within this world.

2. Is there anything that your heart is still clinging to that you know is still of the world? Anything that has been extremely hard to give up? Anything that you know is of the world and not of the Father? What is still capturing your heart about these things?

3. We are in a spiritual battle. What type of sisters and brothers would you want beside you in this battle?

4. How are you being a faithful sister to those alongside you?

From Week 11 Day 2:

5. Day Two spoke of freely worshiping God. What are some of your favorite ways of worshiping God?

Proven Women: The Leader's Guide

> Music, walk in nature, journaling, solitude, conversations about God with others, writing poetry, running, serving others.

6. What are some things that you can commit to do this week to be more intentional about worshiping God?

7. Is there still anything going on in your mind or heart that is keeping you from being able to worship God freely?

> Our heart will never be 100 percent free to worship until heaven. We will always have distractions and some level of pride and selfishness. Some, however, may still be harboring unconfessed sin or consistent sinful habits which are keeping them away from God.

From Week 11 Day 3:

8. Read this quote from *Screwtape Letters*. In this passage, the "Enemy" is referring to God. He writes, "Whenever they are attending to the Enemy Himself we are defeated, but there are ways of preventing them from doing so. The simplest is to turn their gaze away from Him towards themselves. Keep them watching their own minds and trying to produce feelings there by the action of their own wills. When they meant to ask Him for charity, let them, instead, start trying to manufacture charitable feelings for themselves and not notice that this is what they are doing. When they meant to pray for courage, let them really be trying to feel brave. When they say they are praying for forgiveness, let them really be trying to feel forgiven."

   What were your initial thoughts when you read this paragraph?

   > It's scary to think about how accurate his description is to some of our attempts at prayer.

9. How has your prayer life grown throughout the *Study*?

10. Read Matthew 6:5-15 and discuss insights about prayer.

    > We shouldn't pray for attention or to be seen. God already knows what we need before we pray. Jesus gives a model prayer. The different parts of this prayer are seen in the acrostics A.C.T.S. – adoration, confession, thanksgiving, and supplication (praying for requests). All of these should be parts of our prayer.

From Week 11 Day 4:

11. You were asked to look up attributes of God and then write out where you see evidence of these attributes in your life. Does anyone want to share what they wrote?

    In case no one shares, have a few attributes ready and ask them to take a few moments to think about where they see these attributes in their life. Take a few moments to discuss this together as a group.

12. Read a few of these verses as a group and discuss the importance of humility: 1 Peter 5:6, Ephesians 4:2, Philippians 2:14, Philippians 2:4-8, and James 4:6.

13. Why might it be hard to ask God to humble you?

14. Why would it be good for God to humble you?

    Sometimes being humbled can be painful, but it is always for our own good and for His glory.

From Week 11 Day 5:

15. Read Matthew 11:28-30 and discuss what it means to take Jesus' yoke upon you.

    It means to yoke in with Jesus. When I walk with Jesus, He carries the burden on His shoulders. He has already met the perfect standard that I need to be. He is the righteous one. He paid the price for me. He carries the weight on His shoulders. But I do need to walk with Him. I don't get to throw the weight of my sin onto His shoulders, then run away and live my life independent from Him. I come to Him and remain with Him. This is what it means to have a daily walk with the Lord. We walk through life together.

PRAYER

Go around the room having each woman use two verses from Psalm 119 as the content to pray for the woman on her right. Give everyone a turn. Show them how by you starting with 119:1–2, then have someone start with 119:3–4, and so on. Tell the women to take their time in turning the verse into a prayer. Do this until everyone has prayed.

HOMEWORK

Have the women purpose to do something this week that puts another's interests before her own. Tell them to send you a text sharing how it went.

Proven Women: The Leader's Guide

PARTY !!!

Next week is the last week. Decide as a group how you want to celebrate finishing. We can do a pizza party or an ice cream party. This has been a long road so you definitely will want to do something special at the end. Let the ladies know that this last week will be a little different. You will definitely do some discussion, but focus more on celebrating and finishing strong.

SELF-CRITIQUE

Did you allow for full discussion? Did each woman participate?

SEND A TEXT TO THE WOMEN

Have you picked out your next study as this one is nearing its end? I want to encourage you to seriously consider leading another woman through this study as your next step. Otherwise, the pressures of the world will likely keep you from building on the base you are developing. Tell me your plan.

MEMORY VERSE

Ephesians 5:3 "But sexual immorality and all impurity or covetousness must not even be named among you, as is proper among saints."

WEEK  13 (based on Week Twelve *Study* materials)

This is the last scheduled meeting. There is enough material listed to provide a full meeting. Feel free to modify the night by making it a pizza party or ice cream social or whatever. Also, let it be a time of sharing what the women have learned throughout the twelve weeks. You can also hold an additional meeting consisting of just a party. If the women have not shared telephone numbers and email addresses, you can ask the women to share them. They should also select an accountability partner. Be sure to encourage the women to grow, and ask them to consider leading another woman through this study as the next step.

You know your ladies better than any other leader. It is up to you whether you do a full meeting or pizza party or some other time of fellowship. If you do a party and discussion combined, it is up to you and your group whether to start with the party or start with the discussion. Freedom!

OPENING PRAYER

After spending some time greeting one another, open with prayer.

SINGING

Each night, be prepared to sing one song. Let this night be a celebratory song. If you had one song that you did over and over as a theme song, it will be beautiful to do it one last time as a tribute and celebration.

CHECK-IN

Turn to the *Feelings Chart* in Appendix F of the *Study* and check-in. How are they doing tonight and throughout this past week? This is also a good time to see if their emotions changed throughout the duration of the study. Are they more joyful now? Less anxious?

WHAT IMPACTED YOU?

Go around the room and ask each to share:
- What impacted you the most from the twelve weeks we have met together? What are God stories from the entire *Study*? How have they seen God transform their life the most?

LIFETIME PROCESS

Tell the women:
- Healing from sexual sin and living out a Proven life are lifetime processes. We will always be growing and persevering. Freedom is not a one-time or twelve-week event. We must take on an eternal perspective and start viewing each temptation as an opportunity to honor God and to grow.

SETBACKS

Tell the women:
- If you don't feel like a spiritual giant, that is okay. In fact, it's good. When we think we are standing tall, we will fall. Besides, since healing and victory are lifetime processes, we can't expect to be spiritual giants in twelve weeks. The key point is that we keep putting on the armor of God each day, turning to and relying upon Him. We are called each day to walk in the Spirit. We should be growing more and more dependent on God. Not getting better at doing life without Him. It is important to measure each day of our lives by the Word of God, and the six elements of the *PROVEN* acrostic are a great guideline.

Ask:

- Let's review the acrostic: As I say each letter, tell me what it stands for and why it is important for living a Proven life.

    P is for Passionate for God,

    R is for Repentant in spirit,

    O is for Open and honest,

    V is for Victorious in living,

    E is for Eternal in perspective, and

    N is for Networking with other ***Proven Women***.

    Encourage the women to memorize the acrostic and to regularly test their life by it.

MEMORY VERSE

Ask someone to recite the Memory Verse, Ephesians 5:3.

Tell the women: (optional)

- This last week we are going to go through the *Study* a little differently. Instead, we will focus on Psalm 101.

- Read Psalm 101. This starts out with worship and then warns against the things that will pull us away from worship. What do you understand better now than you did twelve weeks ago?

    Spend time discussing the passage.

DISCUSSION QUESTIONS FROM THE *STUDY*

You probably will not have time to discuss all of the questions, so pray through which ones you want to start with. Be willing to be flexible if the Holy Spirit steers the group in a different direction than you planned. These questions are here to be a guide, but feel free to use your own questions as well. These are also optional for this last week since you may also be doing a party.

From Week 12 Day 1

1. How have you seen your heart transform during these twelve weeks?

2. How have you seen God intervene in times of trouble? How have you seen God use it for good?

3. Who is God calling you to comfort, help, or encourage?

From Week 12 Day 2

4. Page 357 lists forms of pride. How can these become temptations when trying to help others?

5. Are you seeing any of these in your life right now?

6. Is becoming a group leader for a future Proven group something that you would consider?

From Week 12 Day 3

7. Did you develop a game plan for cultivating a heart of worship? If so, what is your plan?

8. How have you seen these transform over the past twelve weeks?

    a. Passion for God
    b. Repentant in Spirit
    c. Open and honest
    d. Victorious in living
    e. Eternal perspective
    f. Networking with others

From Week 12 Day 4

9. Read Psalm 119:1-16. How has your life taken a new course?

From Week 12 Day 5

10. What will you be doing to continue this process of intimacy with Christ once this is over?

11. What is your game plan for after this study?

LASTLY

Hopefully you have already heard these ladies share testimonies of how this study has affected them. Give them a last chance to share. Also, challenge them to keep these spiritual disciplines going even after this group ends. How are they going to stay consistent? What do they

Detailed Leader's Guides for All Group Meetings: Week Thirteen

have lined up for their next Bible study and/or community group? Are they willing to become Proven leaders in another woman's life?

God transforms us so that we can both be in a deeper relationship with Him and also so that we can be a light to others. Ask the ladies who they need to be sharing these truths with. Is there someone whom they need to refer to be in a Proven group? Encourage them to find a friend and go through the *Study* with them.

PRAYER

Go around the room, asking each woman to pray what God places on her heart.

HOMEWORK

Be sure to encourage the women to start their next study right away and to never stop being in a daily study for the rest of their lives. It is all about living out a Proven life together with other believers as well as with the Lord. Encourage them to redo this *Study* on their own, and make it an option for some to join in the next group, assuming that you will conduct another.

Suggest that women consider becoming Proven Women small group leaders.

SELF-CRITIQUE

Evaluate how the entire group went, and plan whether you will lead another group. Jot down any notes for making the next group even better. Thank the Lord for this opportunity to lead a group and for His Spirit. Keep praying for the women, and plan to follow up with them. Perhaps you can periodically schedule a picnic or a night of worship. You can also send encouraging notes and continue the practice of hugging them whenever you see them. Above all, make sure that the healing process begun by this Proven group continues to change the lives of the women involved as they draw close to the Lord, receive His power in their lives, and take on His character.

SEND A TEXT TO THE WOMEN

Thank you for attending the group. It was an exciting journey. Don't forget that this is a lifetime process of living out a Proven life. It is vital that you embrace the networking with another woman or all the hard work will soon disappear from your life. Also, be sure to daily test your life against each of the six elements of the PROVEN acrostic.

P is for Passionate for God,

R is for Repentant in spirit,

O is for Open and honest,

V is for Victorious in living,

E is for Eternal in perspective, and

N is for Networking with other Proven Women.

I believe in you!

"Do your best to present yourself to God as one approved, a workman who does not need to be ashamed and who correctly handles the word of truth."
(2 Tim. 2:15)

Congratulations!

Welcome to the Proven Team.

As a graduate we are excited to offer you a special gift to honor your completion of the *Study*.

This will also give you really cool perks throughout our ministry.

Please email, text, or call to receive your gift today.

info@provenmen.org
803-900-3688